Maximizing
Your
Influence
For
Christ

How to be a Servant Leader in Today's World!

(Book 1 of the Servant Leadership Series)

Dr. John F. McGeorge, Jr.

PRESS

Xulon Press
10640 Main Street
Suite 204
Fairfax, VA 22030
(703) 934-4411
XulonPress.com

To order additional copies, call 1-866-909-BOOK (2665).

Other books by Dr. McGeorge

Celebrating God Through Praise & Worship
*Over*coming the Darkness: A Christian Response to the
Cults & Occult

Future books by Dr. McGeorge

Maximum Discipleship/Radical Results: Learning & Living
All the Commandments of Christ [April 2003]
Ultimate Discipleship/Total Results: Learning & Living All
the Commandments of the Apostles [late 2003]
Establishing Your Influence For Christ: Touching the
Home & Church — Book 2 [2004]
Extending Your Influence For Christ: Transforming
Communities & Nations — Book 3 [2005]

Table of Contents

Preface

J esus is constantly calling us to walk in His footsteps as servant leaders at all times. Today's world is witnessing the demise of many leaders who have come to serve themselves and not others like Jesus. Hence, Jesus' challenge to serve and lead is for our generation and every generation. We must face this challenge head-on and make a personal decision that will impact others: will we serve and lead or will we be served and let others lead? Either decision has a lifelong consequence that we will be responsible for; therefore, let us choose to do His will, then the world will see His power, grace, love and truth in full operation by changing lives, cities and nations throughout the world.

Sadly, this has not been the answer most Christians have made. Too many believers throughout history have not taken this challenge seriously, thereby, allowing their nations and future to be damaged spiritually, morally, economically, politically, socially and historically. This book is written with the specific intent to call every believer to accept His challenge before it is too late. This book is also written to motivate all believers to drop the worldly priorities they live by and to learn to live out all the biblical principles of servant leadership as laid out by Jesus and the New Testament

Apostles. If we do, then our generation will greatly bless our society and spare many from innumerable and unnecessary troubles in the future. If we do not, may the Lord forgive and help us in our hour of turmoil that will surely come.

Today, the horizon is filled with many and varied troubles such as natural disasters, economic turmoil, social unrest, political confusion and religious tension on every level that confront us continually. But praise God, this is not the end of the story. This is the beginning of our opportunity to change the direction of our nation in our generation.

This is the first in a series of three books about servant leadership for everyday leaders and believers. This first book lays out the foundational biblical principles of serving and leading as Jesus did, with practical guidance for everyday living. But that is only the beginning. The last two books take these principles further into the everyday life of believers like you and me as we face the daily challenges and tasks of living. Book two builds the walls of these principles for the home and church, elaborating on how they can and should operate on a daily basis in the family and amongst believers in the local fellowships. Finally, book three will build upon the first two books and give overarching principles of how to serve and lead in the larger community where we work and play as well as in the nation where we make political, economic and social decisions that affect us today and tomorrow. Jesus said that we would inherit the earth "if" we followed His principles. These three books seek to explain His will and His ways of servant leadership for every believer.

Jesus' servant leadership affected all areas of life in His generation and every generation thereafter. It is up to you and me to take these principles into our lives and live them out on a daily basis for the benefit and blessing of our families, churches, school, neighborhoods, workplaces, communities and nation at large. The world needs to see these principles in action again and again so that they will once again accuse us of "turning the world upside down" for Christ.

It is clear that He has called you and me to be servant leaders at home, in the church, in the school halls, in the government, as well as in our factories, shops, offices and wherever He has planted us. Therefore, let us be the generation that changes the history of our nation for the Lord and those who will come after us.

Special Formatting

The contents of this book are presented as an aid to help believers grow as servant leaders of Jesus Christ. Too often good books present wonderful materials, but in paragraph form which is not always easy to digest and apply to one's life. Hence, some sections of this book present key principle of servant leadership in short paragraphs in numerical order. This is done to aid learning as follows:

1. It allows the reader to see the concept in a very concise form. This should assist the reader in grasping each new idea.
2. The format enables a reader to comprehend each principle so as to apply it to their personal life.
3. It allows the reader to focus in on one or more principles at a time rather than many ideas simultaneously.

Hopefully, the reader will greatly benefit from this.

Introduction

<u>Serving and Leading</u>

<u>It's Your Style</u>

Servant Leadership is a paradox.
It appears to be a contradiction
in terms. Yet, the "greatest
leader" was a servant who led
through His serving. He gave
all He had to reach all He could
in 3 short years.

Serving and Leading – It's Your God-given Style

Serving and leading are what God has created you to do! Being a servant and leader are what God has created you to be!

Therefore, you are to be a servant leader who should serve and lead all the time!

Your life should be dedicated to learning what it means to be a servant leader like Jesus and nothing less than that. He has created you and me with the ability to be servant leaders in our world. Plus, He has given to all of us the principles that we need to know about how to be excellent servant leaders like Him. That is why this book is dedicated to teaching you how to be the very best servant leader you can be everywhere and everyday.

Today, there are an incredible number of books available on leadership and relatively few on servanthood, which tells us a great deal about how our culture exalts leadership over servanthood. Leading is acceptable, but serving is less desirable. Serving is seen for the weak, while leading is for the strong. Serving is seen for the spiritually poor, while leading is for the aggressive and rich. Serving is seen for those who will never make an impact on their cultures, while leading is for those who do all they can to change people and history. Jesus, however, said that serving is not for any one group of people, but it is the only way to greatness. It was and remains His way to bring about positive and lasting change.

Jesus led from a servant's position, never a ruler's prominence, though He was and is the ruler of all. Consequently, when we serve as He did, we will achieve far more than those who possess the world's power, positions, authority and recognition as leaders. Why? Our impact will be greater because we possess the power of the Holy Spirit living and working in us, a power that no man or organization can duplicate or imitate. For this reason, God has called us to <u>lead by serving</u> so that we can serve by leading; that is the only way for a Christian to live out their life in the fullness of His will.

Some of the books on the market about leadership have been written from a Christian perspective, while others have been written from a secular perspective. A few have been written from a business point-of-view, while countless books have been penned from a political standpoint. More interesting, however, is a select group of books that have been written from a secular perspective, but incorporate Christian principles in hopes of capturing a larger audience. But no matter what the basic perspective of a book may be, many, if not most, of them are written from the perspective of a leader who has power, control or dominance over others because of their position and not something inherent in the person. These authors see the real issue of leadership as a means to gain power or control in order to rule over others. But for believers in Jesus Christ, our perspective is quite different. There **is** something uniquely special and inherent in us: the Holy Spirit. Jesus has all the power and authority in heaven and on earth and He gives it through the Holy Spirit to whomever He desires. Hence, if we serve under His authority and do His will, He shall anoint us with true spiritual power and authority that will transform individuals, families, churches, communities and nations. Captured in this book are the principles that our Lord instituted for our use and benefit in order to be a blessing for others.

Leading from a position of power should not be the goal for Christians or church leaders. Jesus said that the meek, not the weak, shall inherit the earth. His perspective was completely different from the Roman and Jewish rulers of His day, and it was also distinctly contrary to the Zealots and general Jewish expectations of the first century. He gave us a model that worked in His day and has worked in every nation, every society and every place since the first century, but only if and when we employ His principles of servant leadership. But who are the meek? Compare these opposites and see what you glean:

Meek	**not**	weak
Humble	**not**	puffed up
Patient	**not**	intolerant
Submissive	**not**	aggressive
Fair	**not**	biased
Gentle	**not**	harsh

The meek are very strong in Christ because they know, first of all, who they are before God, in Christ, and willingly yield to His will for their lives. Yet, they also appreciate their humble position of total dependence upon Him, and not a position of dominance through Him over others. [Believe me; it is always easier to be a follower than a leader!] Furthermore, servant leaders know how to relate to various types of people and yet consistently reveal His love, grace and truth to everyone. Hence, the meek are those whom He anoints to lead and serve as He did.

For many, serving and leading do not go together because serving occurs when you are at the bottom and leading occurs when you are at the top. They seem to be total opposites cut from different molds and operate from two completely different positions of power and authority. It seems that the two could never work together in a million years. But, just as He empowered the first believers to turn the world upside down spiritually, He can put these seemingly two opposites together in an incredibly dynamic way so that through us He can transform the world all around us everyday and in every way. He can work through you and me to turn our world upside down [or is that right side up?] for Him wherever we are when we commit ourselves to following Him with all of our heart, mind and strength.

Jesus was God in the flesh, the Creator and Judge of all. He was present in the earth to teach the first disciples about the Father and His ways. Even though He was fully God, He willingly laid aside His heavenly powers and privileges in order to reveal to us how to live our lives as servant leaders. His incarnation was for our benefit and blessing in order to bring to us His model of servant leadership to be lived out through us for the blessing and benefit of others as well. He willingly took on the servant model and totally relied upon the Father to empower Him for all that He should do and say. Thus, He has given to us the one true model that will work everyday in every situation without exception. Now that's a positive model for the entire church and world to see and imitate.

Jesus' leadership model rose from the level of a servant because He was endowed with the Holy Spirit as well as abounding in the fullness of truth and grace. He willingly stepped down so that the Father could lift Him up into the full measure of His love, power and truth. He did not seek His own will, nor did He live by His own ways. Instead, just as a servant must rely totally upon their master, Jesus relished in His child-like dependent relationship with the Father before stepping out to minister to others. He did what He saw the Father doing and spoke what He heard the Father saying. So this is **our model** to be emulated in each activity of each day in our lives while on earth.

In this day of political intrigue, economic disaster, and raging wars in many places around the world, countless numbers of peoples are looking for a leader to follow. Of course, they can readily choose the brutal leaders who seek to destroy their opponents, overthrow political rulers, and do everything they can to obtain power and authority by force. Or they could join the ever-increasing numbers who are delving into the cultic world of the supernatural. But for Jesus, that is not the way He lived and nor should it be ours. He wants to instill in you and me the principles of servant leadership that can lead others out of darkness into His marvelous light, out of bondage into the freedom in the Spirit and out of death into His everlasting life.

Jesus' model comes from a pure spiritual perspective. It comes from the Father who originally entrusted the world to Adam and Eve. He placed them in His garden as His ambassadors to rule over all of His creation, yet they had to remain under His authority while in relationship with Him in order to be effective. If they ever disregarded that relationship and all the blessings that it could bring, then they and all future generations were in terrible trouble. We all know the story that Adam and Eve blew it royally, but Jesus came to redeem and restore what they had lost and destroyed. Today, and everyday for that matter, the greatest, most effective, and enduring model of living is the servant leader model that can transform life all around us.

Because a servant leader is on the bottom of life, they are not trying to develop plans to force upon others. In fact, a servant leader doesn't need to cultivate plans and strategies, which in turn frees up their mind and spirit to focus in on understanding the perspective of others around them. Likewise, because they are at the bottom of life they are totally dependent upon the Father for all things pertaining to life and godliness, and they are only as effective as they allow the anointing to flow in, out, and through them. Therefore, this book will seek to explore the biblical perspective of servant leadership that all believers should live by, whether you are a parent, child, educator, mechanic, clerk, politician, businessperson, or church leader. Jesus has an exciting role for you and me to carry out in His kingdom. Your role, as a servant leader, will transform your life and the lives of those you touch through your actions and words.

Key Principle

A servant leader sees through spiritual eyes.
A servant leader hears through spiritual ears.
A servant leader senses through a
spiritual heart.
And a servant leader discerns through a
spiritual mind.

A servant leader has the best of all worlds. They have the calling, covering, and gifting from the Father, while at the same time they have the opportunity, invitation, and possibilities to reach out into a spiritually starving world that is crying out for leaders and servants. Servant leaders should be filled and surrounded with His life and opportunities in order to instill His life in others.

Servant leadership is not easy, but it is very rewarding, both now and in eternity. Servant leadership does not necessarily involve quick action and change, but the laying of progressive patterns that will slowly transform the hearts and minds of mankind while re-establishing His principles in the cultural beliefs of a nation. Becoming a servant leader is a lifetime commitment that you and I will continually grow into, and through time and effort we will change the destiny of people and nations.

History is wrought with living examples of godly men and women who came to serve and lead just as Jesus did. They came to build the truth in their nations through the power and grace of the Holy Spirit, which subsequently brought about significant change for people and nations in time. Let us launch into this study with an expectation of hearing what the Spirit is saying to His people so that they can be excellent servant leaders just like Jesus.

Part I

<u>Why A Servant?</u>

Serving others is a great
honor and privilege
for any believer
who loves Jesus.
Jesus set the example
for all believers to follow—
to love our neighbors by serving
them as much as we
love and serve ourselves.

Why a Servant Before a Leader?

Everyone wants to be a leader! But, not everyone wants to be a servant! If you want to be a leader like Christ, that's probably why you are reading this book. But what about wanting to be a better servant? Since He has called you and me to both positions, then we should want to be better servants and leaders, not one or the other. Besides, the two go together in God's economy and cannot be separated; if you try, you will lose the benefit of both. Therefore, seek to be a better servant and leader simultaneously and you will excel in both positions.

Maybe you want to be a better family leader, or church leader, or a better leader on your job or in your school, or you just want to learn more about good leadership qualities and principles so that you can incorporate them into your daily life and ministry. No matter where you are a leader, you can grow as a leader as you build His servant principles into your beliefs, attitudes, style, and behavior. You can and will mature as a leader "**IF**" you choose to follow His servant principles. So the goal is to become the very best leader possible **"WHEN"** you integrate God's servant principles in this book into your life and ministry.

The natural question is which should we focus on first, leadership or servanthood? Which of the two is the foundational principle that controls the growth and development of the other? Why does one have priority over the other? Why has God established a particular order for them to be effective? What if we violate His order, will that really affect how we serve and lead? These are legitimate questions that you need to ask and have answered. Furthermore, we need to know if we are called to be a leader or a servant first in life? What if I am the head of my family, or head of my school or job, church or community? Can't I be a leader without having to be a servant? Why should we want to be a servant at all if the possibility of being a leader is open to us? Besides, being a servant is definitely not rewarding; it is the lowest, dirtiest, and least respected job in the whole world. Servants do not have any status, importance, or significance, and they are usually treated with indifference at best. It is by far more exciting and rewarding to be a leader. You will be recognized by your position, which carries the stamp of importance, and you will also have the luxury of exercising power as the leader. But is that God's best for you, that is, being a leader or being a servant? The answers you give to these questions will reveal a great deal about who you are, where you are spiritually, what you hope to achieve in life and how you expect to achieve your goals. It will reveal whether or not you are walking in tune with His Spirit.

The greatest person in all of history, Jesus Christ, was a servant first and foremost. Even though He came as a servant, He had the requisite power, wisdom, vision, and love that flowed from heaven into and out of His being to all people in various circumstances around Him. He made a difference not only in the first century, but also in every century since His incarnation through believers like you and me who fully follow His will and ways. If we will only serve as He did, we too will have a similar impact upon our societies and nations through our servant leadership. Why? Because service releases God's potential in and through our life to hear what He is saying and see what He is doing so that we can accomplish what He wants done.

The Apostle Paul impacted his world then, and we are still experiencing that impact today through his epistles. Leaders who serve first and foremost seek to walk in Jesus' steps, allowing the Holy Spirit to fully and freely work through them in order to impact people, circumstances, and situations around them. Look at Watchman Nee and how he almost single-handedly changed China. Or look at John Wesley and how he touched England and saved them from the brink of war, brought revival to a spiritually dry land, and started a worldwide movement that is still with us today. And look at Billy Graham in our day: his servant leadership has literally been used by God to bring millions into the Kingdom all around the world. These are only a few of the hundreds and thousands of examples of servant leaders that are changing the history of peoples and nations.

But there is more to this story than meets the eye. In the world's scheme of things, servants are considered worthless, and that's why Paul once referred to himself as the 'scum of the earth' [1 Cor. 4:13]. But, in God's eyes His servants are infinitely valuable to Him and those whom they serve whether they acknowledge it or not. In fact, you and I are so valuable that He has stamped His very image into your being as the stamp of ownership. Christ sees God's image in us and directs His Spirit to teach us, empower us, refresh us, encourage us, guide us, correct us, discipline us, and guide us along life's path to fulfill all that He has for us! Now that's a fulfilled life simply by being a servant of Jesus Christ.

But you say, "How can He see any good in me? I sin. I

lie. I'm lazy. I gossip. I cheat on my taxes. I don't love others as He does. I watch bad things on TV. Besides, I have evil thoughts. I see value in other people but certainly not in myself. I think my life is fairly useless and no one cares anyway, so He couldn't possibly use me. Plus, it's less likely that He would love me if He really knew what is in me." Don't you just feel that way sometimes? I do. It seems that all of life is against you or at least not on your side. But, again, there is more to your life's story than meets the eye!

He loves you **because** He wants to love you and He willingly makes a personal choice to love you everyday. But, He also loves you for five very specific and conscious reasons on His part. (1) He created you in His image, period and because He loves Himself, He naturally loves you. (2) He created you to fellowship with Him and longs to commune with you. (3) He created you to rule the earth, so He wants to communicate His will to you so that you will be as effective as Jesus was during His earthly ministry. (4) He created you to live together in community with His people in the peace and love of the Holy Spirit. And (5) He created you to win people to salvation as well as crush the power and works of the evil one [see 1 John 3:8]. Therefore, His multi-dimensioned love for you is beyond your ability to comprehend, but it's always there.

In many ways, you and I are similar to God in our spirit and soul. Of course, God is Spirit and we remain different from Him in many eternal ways, but there are similarities. Yet, this is not the main problem we are dealing with. The key problem lies in the fact that sin has covered up and distorted His image in us as well as distorted our ability to think and believe clearly. Unfortunately, many believers would rather believe a lie than His truth, all to their detriment. Too many believers see themselves as sinners under grace, but God sees us as saints indwelt by the Holy Spirit because we are the "temple" of the Holy Spirit. He sees the positive while too many of us see the negative, which is regrettable.

Let me ask you this simple question: when Paul wrote His various letters, did he write to the saints or to the sinners? He always wrote to the saints who needed further sanctification; if he had written to the sinners, they would still need salvation. So which are you: a sinner needing salvation or a saint needing further sanctification? You are saved, redeemed by the blood, indwelt by His Spirit, growing in grace and the knowledge of the truth. Consequently, walk in His truth with the joy and freedom of the Holy Spirit, which is positive, liberating, and uplifting. His love is so great for you, that He has gone to great lengths to restore the damaged image in you through His salvation. Plus, He has promised to work with and in you until you are whole, complete, blameless, spotless, and cleaned up into the fullness of His image again. If you will recognize and accept this by faith as His eternal truth, then you will walk in His peace, joy, and comfort forevermore. You will know that even when you sin and foul things up royally, He will redeem you and cause your failings to work to your good and for the good of others in time.

A Servant Who Cares

Have you ever wondered why there are so many commands in the Bible? Perhaps you wish that they weren't there, or that He would at least give us an option as to which ones we must follow. From beginning to end, the Bible has hundreds of positive commands about how we are to relate to God, our neighbors, and others. However, there are also countless negative commands, especially in the New Testament. Why did He give us both and not just the positive commands? Take a look at just a few of the negative ones:

• Do not judge one another [Romans 14:13]

- Do not be arrogant on behalf of one against another [I Cor. 4:6]
- Do not have law suits with one another [I Cor. 6:7]
- Do not deprive one another in marriage [I Cor. 7:5]
- Do not bite and devour one another [Gal. 5:15]
- Do not consume one another [Gal. 5:15]
- Do not challenge one another [Gal. 5:26]
- Do not envy one another [Gal. 5:26]
- Do not lie to one another [Col. 3:9]
- Do not repay one another with evil [I Thess. 5:15]
- Do not hate one another [Titus 3:3]
- Do not speak against one another [Jas. 4:11]
- Do not complain against one another [Jas. 5:9]
- Do not stop being hospitable with one another [I Pet. 4:9]

So why all of these negative ones?

The answer is quite simple: He wants to establish firm borders for our life and ministry. The negative commands tell us where the limits are while the positive commands tell us how to live and minister within the borders He has established.

God has created all people in His image [see James 3:9]. Not only is it stamped into our personality, but it is also part of our inward nature, though our sinful acts and desires often hide it. This is why we have such internal conflicts within ourselves at times: we are acting, thinking, desiring or doing something against the very nature of God in us. Therefore, whenever we speak, think, or act against another person in an ungodly way, we are speaking, thinking, or acting against God's image in that person and it should bother us because we are violating God's goodness in us. For these reasons, He has given us an extensive list of "do's and do not's" so that we will not harm the image of God in another person or ourselves. The positive and negative commands go hand-in-hand: the positive ones help us to focus on His will in order to move towards His goals for our life and ministry, while the negative ones help us to avoid error and set up boundaries that we should not cross.

A Christian leader should be a better servant than other leaders, especially when compared with the standard set by non-Christians. A good leader, however, knows their own weaknesses, but seeks to capitalize on their strengths while minimizing their weaknesses. And a good leader looks to Christ as the living example, seeking to replicate the characteristic of being a servant first and foremost.

What a Servant Should Expect

Expectations are a part of life. You have expectations about yourself, your spouse, your children, others you associate with, life, the future, your home, job, and what you hope to achieve before you die. Likewise, servant leaders should have certain expectations about themselves, their calling and ministry everyday. They should have short-term and long-term expectations. They should also have daily expectations as well. This is important because our life and ministry expectations give us goals to work towards. So from His perspective, we should take all expectations seriously. However, we must be sure that our expectations are His, are reasonable, possible and within the realm of His calling upon our life.

Expectations can be positive motivators to spur us on to excellence in our servant leadership roles. Likewise, expectations, whether yours or someone else's, can be either good or bad. It all depends on whether or not the expectations conform to God's will. For example, a husband or wife should have clear and detailed expectations of their marriage; otherwise, disaster is just around the corner. There is nothing wrong with expressing one's expectations with another, especially in the home, church and work place. This is quite natural and predictable. However, problems arise when either (1) those expectations are either unexpressed or unclear, or (2) the expectations are unrealistic and drive us or others like a harsh taskmaster, which is not the way of Jesus Christ. He said, "My yoke is easy, and My load light" [Matt. 11:30]. Therefore, anytime we come under the pressure of expectations that are out of the Spirit's will and ways, we will gradually slip out from under grace and come under the burden of the flesh, which is cruel and never satisfied. Take for example a husband's expectation that his wife will be a "super-woman/mom/helper," yet she turns out to be less than he "expected." He has created an unbearable and unrealistic load for her to carry. No matter what she does, she will never measure up because the expectations are (1) unrealistic, (2) unnatural, (3) don't allow her the grace to fail and grow, and (4) probably outside of the realm of her ability to fulfill. This results in him becoming frustrated easily, disappointed with even her best achievements, and angry that she can't measure up. Furthermore, it creates an air of uncertainty in her life, fear of failure, physical and emotional turmoil not to speak about her growing inability to relate to her husband. It shouldn't be that way; chaos is not of the Father, but love, peace, and joy are. When our expectations are constantly frustrated, we need to re-evaluate them in order to see if they are Christ-like or not. If they are Christ-like, they will be gentle, but if not, they will be burdensome beyond comparison and overwhelming, which shouldn't be the case. This would be a sad state of affairs.

Expectations motivate us to do what He wants us to do as well as restrain us from evil. Since we naturally establish expectations for others and ourselves, we will expect them to be fulfilled. But when they are not, there is an immediate letdown in our spirit which ushers in irritation and growing disappointment in us, questions arise in our mind, and a natural "why" relentlessly plagues us day and night. Why didn't it happen? Why didn't I measure up? Why can't they just get it? The "why" questions go on and on.

God has created us in such a way that our expectations should flow from His heart, not ours. When they do, there will be a natural peace in our life, which will rule and overrule chaos and unrealistic desires. His expectations are spirit and life, whereas our expectations so often are fleshly and self-centered. He has given us His general expectations in the Word, but specific expectations for each individual must come through the still small voice of His Spirit speaking into our spirit on a regular basis. This requires us to stop and listen to the voice of the Lord regularly; otherwise, we will continue down a path of self-imposed expectations and frustrations.

Because we are part of His Kingdom, servant leaders should have expectations that conform to the calling, ministry, and position that He has placed us in. Therefore, let us look at some general expectations for all servant leaders. Each servant leader should expect:

1. **To be viewed as a slave or servant of others**. This may seem to make us less than worthy, but Jesus, too, was a servant to all and yet God exalted Him far above every name in heaven and earth.

2. **To be called a slave or servant**. Not a very flattering title is it? But, it has a rich reward. Being called a servant or slave of Christ for the service of others is a badge of honor in His eyes. Therefore, be proud of this God-given title.

3. **To develop a servant's attitude and behavior.**
This puts our life, word, family, and future in quite
a different light. It will take us time to learn the biblical attitudes and behavior He has proscribed for us,
to examine our present attitudes and behavior, to
repent of what is already wrong and begin to build
into our spirit and mind the right attitudes and
behavior. This is the process of sanctification or
spiritual growth that every believer should go
through regularly.

4. **To learn God's will specifically for them, and
then to do it from the heart.** This will take time
and commitment on your part. But the good news is
this: He has already given us His commands as well
as His demands for our life. Hence, a good servant
leader will love God with their mind by studying His
Word regularly in order to know His will and ways.

5. **To learn what are the rights, privileges and
responsibilities of a servant.** Rights and privileges
are balanced with personal responsibilities. Of
course learning one's rights and privileges sound
great, but we must carefully examine our responsibilities as well. If we want to walk in full obedience
to His Word, then learning responsibilities mean that
we are obligated to fulfill the expectations and duties
given to us by the Lord of all.

6. **To serve others often, and to look for opportunities
to use their God-given talents for the benefit and
blessing of others.** Servants are outward looking, not
inwardly focused. Many of today's personal problems
stem from the fact that people are so self-focused that
they forget that they can grow and overcome barriers

by using the God-given talents for the good of others. If we focus on others, many of our problems will naturally dissolve into nothing, and the reward for serving others will more than overwhelm our spirit and mind.

7. **Hardship, mistreatment, misunderstanding, persecution, and challenges from others to compromise our commitment to Christ.** A servant of Christ will shine into the darkness of the world's ways, causing those in the darkness to bark and bite back. But not to worry, He has overcome the world and this "Overcomer" lives in us. That is why we can proclaim with full assurance, "greater is He who lives in us than he who lives in the world."

8. **To be tempted to give up on being a servant because it's too hard, especially when you serve the undeserving and ungrateful.** Sometimes, after a particularly difficult period, servant leaders would prefer to throw in the towel and join the crowd, chasing after power, position, and prestige rather than constantly bowing down in humble servitude to others. It certainly looks more rewarding, but believe me, it isn't. The devastation of abandoning our call far outweighs any momentary benefits derived from fleeing the pressures. So stand firm as Paul told us to in Ephesians 6.

9. **To study God's word in depth, to read quality and in-depth Christian literature, learn His truth completely and the principles contained therein.** I once had a publisher tell me that most Christian books that are published are novels written on an eighth grade level. Now that's pathetic! How in the

world are we ever going to transform the nations with humanistic romance novels or substandard truth? It will never happen. A lazy or ignorant servant leader is a sad contradiction. Servant leaders by nature, calling, and demand must know their Master personally and in-depth, know His will and carry it out on a regular basis.

10. **To pray and fast regularly.** Our flesh is truly weak and it wants to dominate our spirit much of the time. However, fasting and praying denies the flesh its control, subdues it, and opens our spirit and mind to hear the voice of the Spirit to know and do His will. Servant leaders must grow not only in grace, but also in their relationship with the Father. Hence, prayer and fasting should be a normal part of who we are and what we do.

11. **To show respect for those in authority over them as well as to submit to them**. This is not always easy, especially when the authority is corrupt, immoral, ungodly, harsh, or uncaring. However, the power of the Holy Spirit in a servant leader can overcome the power of every unrighteous and ungodly person and plan, and give them the ability to love their masters even when they are so undeserving. So when we respect and submit to any authority in a godly way, we show forth our love for God.

12. **To guard their heart and mind.** The heart and mind are the gateway to our spirit and soul. Therefore, we need to guard them from ungodliness in whatever form it may come. TV, movies, music and the like are some of the strongest influences for evil or good in our society. Most of this does not glo-

rify God. Besides, Jesus warned us to be careful to what we listen to [Mark 4:24]. His Word says to be filled with His Spirit and let the Word of God richly dwell within you, that is, influence your every thought, desire, will and way [Col. 3:16]. Now that's true eternal wealth.

13. **To serve others spiritually**. It is crucial that our service either adds to or corrects what may be deficient in the faith of others. When we add to what they already know and live, then we are helping to build up others spiritually, intellectually, morally and emotionally [Phil. 2:30]. Christ wants maturing servant leaders in His kingdom, so we should expect to devote a great deal of time to developing others.

14. **To seek out opportunities to serve**. Our call is to seek to serve anyone, whether at home, in the community, work place, school, etc. Servants were created to serve, and a Christian servant should find joy and fulfillment in serving others just as Jesus did. Sometimes opportunities will simply come our way, but we are to be actively seeking to use our talents for others. Look at the cults and ungodly religious movements; they are constantly seeking or creating opportunities to influence others, so why should we do anything less? Christ sought the Father who guided Him by the Spirit into those opportunities to glorify His name.

15. **Establish godly priorities in our life**. God has established a divine order of priorities, which we must follow. They are according to God's will: first is the Lord, second is the family, third is the job of providing for one's family, fourth is the church and

His people, and everything else follows from there. Right priorities and a good balance in those priorities will keep a servant leader on track.

16. **To be open, honest and clean before God.** To maintain a clear conscience and pure motives before, during, and after serving others. Motives are very important; therefore, godly servants regularly examine themselves spiritually to be sure that their motives line up with His Word. This is one evidence of a maturing servant leader [see I Cor. 2:15].

17. **To maintain an attitude of humility.** Servant leaders should try to be humble in all matters, even when wronged. Humility has often been maligned as a sign of weakness, but Christian humility is a sign of maturity and strength. Jesus served others in and through His humility, and so should we.

18. **To stand for what is right and godly without compromise.** Silence may be one of the easiest forms of compromise, therefore, a servant leader should not be lulled into silence whether out of fear for their safety or desire to maintain peace at all cost. God has established a standard for all to follow, so let every servant leader take their stand for God and His way no matter what.

Servant leaders should seek to know and establish His expectations in their life and ministry. When they conform their expectations to His, then the natural results will be life-giving to others. This is what He wants from every servant leader, to be a life-giver to the lost and dying world around us so as to transform it by His Spirit and Word.

What a Servant Shouldn't Expect

Moving on to the next step, it is also good for servant leaders to have specific expectations of what should not be or happen. We could call these "negative expectations" because they should not occur. When a servant leader knows what they are, then they can focus on where the legitimate boundaries lie. This balance between "positive expectations" that define what we should expect and "negative expectations" that define what we should not expect will enable every servant leader to function within clearly defined boundaries of godly service and leadership. Furthermore, having the positive and negative expectations will also keep a servant leader attuned to what they should avoid so as to prepare them to reject the negative should it ever arise in their presence.

When a servant leader lives within the realm of what is expected and does not attempt to have or develop expectations outside of this realm, their life and service will be far more enjoyable and effective. Servant leaders are to live a life in service for others as directed by the Holy Spirit through the giftings and talents that He has given to each one of us. For this reason, there are some things that a servant leader should never expect to do or happen, but if they do, then the occurrence will allow them to exercise wisdom and discernment in rejecting it. Servant leaders should not expect:

1. **To be in charge as a leader**. They are called to serve, and if a leadership position is given to them, praise God for His advancement in this way. Anyone who "wants" to lead is probably seeking power and prestige through a position. Watch out for that person because they don't have a servant's heart!

2. **To be #1, or even close to it, in anything**. A servant is not #1, but #0, last, at the bottom of the pile. The old saying, "You need to look out for #1," is the world's way of putting self before others. However, our saying is to look out for opportunities to serve #1 who are others and not ourselves.

3. **To be served by others**. A servant's focus is more outward than inward, thus always looking for opportunities to serve others. Servant leaders find fulfillment and personal pleasure in serving others, so that is one of the reasons they love to serve people. Never expect others to serve you, but if they do, accept it as a special blessing from above.

4. **To be revered, feared, or lifted above others**. It is God who exalts man, not man by himself. When man exalts himself, pride and arrogance blinds them to the need to serve others and builds within them the demand to be served, which is completely unlike Jesus. Servant leaders are like Jesus, they seek to

care for or meet the needs of others instead of drawing attention to themselves.

5. **To know the future**. The Lord may give us insight or hints of what's to come at times, but our future is always to serve others without necessarily knowing what lies around the corner. Keep in mind that if when a servant leader serves, they are preparing others for the future, whatever that may be.

6. **To profit financially from serving**. The New Testament is replete with commands and directives to pay Christ's laborers, but this should never be the reason for serving others. Their goal always remains to serve, help, benefit, aid, assist and sustain others through their loving care. As a side note, it is sad and devastating when the body of Christ does not properly care for its own laborers. For example, most churches expect them to always serve without compensation. However, Paul debunked that myth in I Cor. 9 where he states that a laborer is worthy of their wage. As long as the church refuses to follow His word, it will be to its own detriment and that of the world around her.

7. **To function independently from Christ or the body of Christ**. Since He created us to live in community, we really do need one another. Nothing comes from within us, but from the Father of all glory, who gives us everything pertaining to life and godliness. Therefore, we should walk humbly together because He is our source for everything in the visible and invisible realms.

8. **To be recognized by anyone for anything they do.**

Jesus said that even "when you do all the things which are commanded you, say, 'We are unworthy slaves; we have done only that which we ought to have done" [Luke 17:10]. Now that's humbling to say the least. We seek no recognition but the reward of serving others.

9. **To be rewarded for our serving**. Again, rewards are not the goal but a blessed by-product "if" they come. But even if they don't come, our reward is the joy of serving others and eternal glory in eternity. Too many ministries today focus on financial rewards, which contradict Paul's emphasis on having "all the spiritual blessings" in the here and now as articulated by Paul in Eph. 1:3ff.

10. **To advance beyond the position of a servant**. "Once a servant, always a servant" is our motto. Those who look for a position are looking beyond Christ who is our head. If He is the head, then why are we attempting to advance ourselves? We should be looking for opportunities, not positions. The sons of Zebedee tried that, but Jesus only rebuked them for that [Matt. 20:20ff]. Jesus will promote us in the here and now on the basis of faithful service in fulfilling our callings and opportunities and not on the basis of our desires or seeking to have a position.

11. **Living and serving to be easy or without problems**. We are in the "people business" and that is never easy. People have different demands, personalities, expectations, desires, pasts, hurts, and so on. Hence, when we attempt to live as a servant and serve others, they see us through their life's prism

and it may distort things from time to time and cause us unnecessary pain. Peter saw Jesus through a prism of selfishness and attempted to stop Him from going to the cross. Even though this may have been painful, the final fruit was good.

12. **To find comfort all the time.** Comfort is a natural desire of our flesh, especially if we can avoid uncomfortable physical surroundings or personal/interpersonal encounters. There is nothing wrong with comfort in and of itself, but when that becomes the goal, then we will unfortunately exclude opportunities to step down into the lifestyles of those whom He may have called us to serve.

13. **Praise from others.** Do not seek praise from our various "authorities," be it in the family, church, community, work place, school, or anywhere else. Every believer desires and needs encouragement, but we should never expect it. Growing and maturing servants must encourage themselves, and this can only be done if they know Him well. But when praise comes, give the glory to Him who empowered you to do what you did as an ambassador of Christ.

14. **To retire from serving.** Our life of service is endless because it is a lifetime commitment and function. Because He owns us, He has the right to dictate how long we are to serve; from His perspective, it is life long. Retirement is not Biblical, but service is. Therefore, expect to serve all your life, even if you slow down as you age.

15. **Excessive leisure time to do as you please.** Jesus did take time to rest and seek refreshment, and

servant leaders should do the same in order to maximize their effectiveness and life span. But that is not our main priority; leisure is not the name of the game, but serving is.

16. **Honor from the world**. This is neither our goal nor desire because we will probably receive indifference at best and attacks at worse. If the world honors us, be careful because the world's standards don't measure up to Christ's. But if it happens, take the opportunity to serve the world by telling them about the One who enabled you to serve them.

17. **Problem-free relationships**. We are under grace and growing in different ways and at different rates. Personalities will come into conflict, ideas will clash, and opinions will rage against one another from time-to-time, so relationships will be strained because we aren't perfect yet. Servant leaders should accept that "there must also be factions, among you, in order that those who are approved may have become evident among you" [I Cor. 11:19]. This is God's way of approving His servants and disapproving the arrogant and independent and self-sufficient ones whom He rejects.

18. **To have all wisdom and knowledge.** This would be nice, but no one individual believer has all wisdom, knowledge, or answers for the questions and situations that you will face. Servants are not "all sufficient," but He is. When we lack wisdom, desire, strength, moral fortitude, and so forth, we can humble ourselves before Him and ask for more of Him, to change our desires and renew us in and through His word and Spirit who gives life.

19. **To have a fear of people.** We are called to serve others and to serve under others. Therefore, if a fear of people is in your life, it exists only because we make them out to be more than they really are. That is, we make them into living idols to which our emotions and thoughts bow down. People are just people like you and me. Maybe they have a more dynamic character, powerful position, strong personality, loud voice, money, or something else, but it doesn't matter because they are made up of the same parts like you and me: spirit, soul and body.

20. **To shrink from service.** We should never be afraid to step out in faith to serve whomever, wherever or whenever He leads us. Faith is the strength to overcome and control our fears so that we can move forward in His will. Fear is a function of a lie controlling our spirit and mind; but faith is His power to direct our believing and thinking.

21. **Anyone to stand up for them or their rights.** Put downs are the norm for servants, so when we are offended, abused, misused or victimized, then we should not expect anyone to stand up for us. Sometimes we have to do it for ourselves; but if someone does stand up for and with us, then praise the Lord. Keep in mind that He is for us, in us, and with us always [Romans 8].

22. **To be free to live how we desire.** Freedom is not doing anything we want, but doing what is right and spiritually healthy. Freedom has restraints; otherwise, if there were no restraints at all we would have chaos and slavery, not freedom. Furthermore, we have an obligation to Him and a calling upon our life

to serve where He plants us till He moves us.

23. **To fail in our calling or serving**. None of us are perfect, but sin should not be a looming factor hanging over us or operating in us. Likewise, we should not be unfaithful in fulfilling His calling upon our life. In the New Testament, Christians are not called sinners, but saints. Therefore, a saint has the same anointing as Christ did, so how can we fail? We only fail if we refuse to follow Him and His desires.

24. **To be first in the eyes of man**. We are already first in the eyes of Christ, and what the world thinks or sees should be irrelevant. Only God can see with perfect vision into our life and situations, so His praise and status far outweighs anything that the world could ever offer.

25. **To be well received by the world**. When we live and speak as He desires, the world will reject us because our message, lifestyle, and truth contradict and rub against the world's ways, will, and plans. The world is not our friend, He is. Therefore, we need to maintain a strong friendship with Him and His people.

26. **To be compared to others, whether by ourselves or by others**. Some Christians have a bad habit of comparing themselves to others, either trying to measure up or stand taller than all others around them. This should not be the case for servant leaders. He knows us better than anyone else does and how to measure our progress. Besides, if we compare ourselves to one another, confusion will reign, which is neither His will or way [2 Cor. 10:12].

27. **To be lazy**. The Holy Spirit energizes and emboldens us to serve others energetically. When He speaks His "rhema," that is, His personal Word to us, it should delight us to know that when He speaks to us personally as a Father does to His child, He is empowering us to serve.

28. **To keep all their money to themselves, or stop tithing and giving offerings**. Money is only a passing "thing" in this world. He tests us through money to see where our heart is. We should be faithful to tithe and give offerings, care for our family, and support the work of Christ. So, our hands should be open so that He may pour an abundance into our life to help and assist others [see Malachi 3:7ff]

Key Principle

We give up our claims to fame, fortune, and the future in order to receive from Him direction, dictates, and demands upon our life to serve others. Sounds hard, but in reality it is very easy and truly enjoyable for those who follow Him with all their heart, mind, and body.

What A Servant Gives Up

Being a servant of Christ **is** a great privilege. Christ the King invites us to come to Him, to sit at His feet to learn how to serve just as He did. But, just as it cost Christ everything to become a servant, it will cost you and me everything as well. Christ gave up His power, position, comfort, control and prestige in order to come to earth in the flesh so that He could live and serve as an example for you and me [see Philippians 2:1-9]. Instead of holding on to what He had, He released it all in order to achieve the goal of redemption for all mankind. The result of His serving was that "God highly exalted Him, and bestowed on Him the name which is above every name." This is the direct result of His obedience in giving up what was necessary in order to receive what was indispensable for a true Servant. He gave up all in order to serve all, which resulted in the greatest service ever performed on earth. Now we, too, must follow in His footsteps to serve as He served.

> ## <u>Key Principle</u>
>
> We give up what we will lose before we lose it in order to gain what we cannot lose for all eternity. And our gain is everyone else's reward because the life-giving Spirit that lives in the heart of servant leader like you and me will give His life as a service to all through us.

Our cost, therefore, is not small. It is great, and every true servant of Christ should carefully consider what they must personally give up, and then decide if it is worth it or not, and if they are willing or not to give it up, permanently. Jesus teaches us this principle through a parable about building a tower or fighting a war. Luke 14:25-35 speaks about "calculating the cost" before building, or "taking counsel" before you commit to the fight. It is the same with us as servant leaders. We must weigh in the balance all factors before we decide whether or not we are willing to give up all that He asks in order to carry out all that He commands of us. We should take counsel from other mature Christians about this very weighty decision before we make a final commitment to Him. Once we make the choice and accept the responsibility of a servant leader, there is no looking back, no recalculating the cost, and no asking out of the obligation. It's like joining the army, once you join it, you're in whether you like it or not. So let us carefully and methodically count the costs and decide intelligently what we will do.

Here is a list of the minimal cost of being a servant leader. Since you are probably already a believer, you may want to evaluate your present life against the demands of being a full-blown servant leader of Christ, and see how you measure up, and make any necessary changes in order to maximize your service and leadership. A servant leader will have to give up:

1. **Control over their life**. Who's in charge of your time, talent, and possessions? Everything we have from the day we are born to the day we die comes from Him. Therefore, Christ asks each of us to let Him be Lord over all of our life, including our time, possessions, comfort, protection, family, job, relationships and future. Giving up control over anything in our life is very difficult for most, especially those of us who are "control freaks." However, giving Him control has enormous rewards for our life; we will have His peace, His comfort when we are in trouble, His provision for our needs, His wisdom for every situation, His power under control, and so forth. "His power has given to us everything pertaining to life and godliness" [II Pt. 1:3], therefore, what more is there? We have it all, so let us lay aside our lusts for the things of this world and cling to the spiritual blessings He has invested already in us.

2. **Insisting on their rights**. Everyone has rights, and as a lawyer, I understand the importance of protecting ones rights in the face of those who would steal or abuse our rights. But, as a member of the Kingdom, how we view our rights is quite different. Each believer has many legal rights protected by law, and we can also say that we have many spiritual rights guaranteed by our Lord. But, here is where the conflict comes in: something good or bad happens to, or against us, and we have the right to protest and proceed against someone for what has happened. What do we do? This is where our heart

is really revealed. Do we insist on our rights that they must always be protected and promoted, or do we carefully judge the situation and decide what is best for us and others involved? Blind rights see only what "I" deserve rather than what is best for everyone. A true servant of Jesus will not insist on getting their rights every time, but they will weigh all things in the balance and make a godly decision.

3. **Protecting their reputation**. Reputation is everything for too many people and it usually involves how we perceive what others see in us, whether it is good or bad. Most people want everyone to think good of them, no matter what. The result is that people like this are "people-pleasers," even if they are believers. People-pleasers want their reputation upheld because it is the center of their focus. There is no question that our reputation is important, but only to a limited degree. When it becomes the focal point of our relationships, then our relationships become very self-serving. However, as a servant of Jesus, we are to lay aside our reputation just as Jesus did, and do what is right even if it isn't popular. Christ guards our reputation. His opinion of us is more important than anyone else's opinion, period.

4. **Holding claim to our possessions as solely our own**. The early church was so filled with the Holy Spirit that people leapt for the opportunity to sell their goods in order to serve and assist others. Christ has given to each of us many possessions, but they are placed in our hands as stewards, not as primary owners. Jesus remains the primary owner of all that we have or ever will have. Therefore, as stewards we are under authority to use our possessions as He

commands us for the service of others. Keep in mind, however, that we are to love others as we love ourselves. So if we care for ourselves through our possessions, we must equally care for others with our possessions also.

5. **Right to set our own agenda.** We are to set priorities in our life through understanding His general Word ["logos" from the Bible] and His specific Word spoken to us through the Holy Spirit ["rhema"]. However, our agenda is really set by Him because His agenda is our agenda. It is not our agenda that must become His agenda. He placed man and woman on the earth to rule over the earth for Him. Therefore, we need to know both His specific and general will for the short-term as well as the long-term. Hence, if we should disobey or rebel against God's chosen will for our life, we will sadly miss the impact that He wants us to have on others. But, since we are not perfect, we are to fulfill it to the degree that He gives us the ability to do it.

6. **Right to be proud of who I am and what I accomplish.** There is a good pride and a bad pride. Good pride looks at all that He has enabled you to do, and rejoices in Him and our God-given abilities, giving Him the full credit for it. Bad pride looks at all that you have done and takes heart that you are an accomplished person. The subtle difference is who is at the center of our focus, Christ or me? As a servant, I give up the right to claim credit for any good I have, can, or will do. But, if I am honored for serving like Him, then I will humbly accept the gratitude and point everyone back to Him who is the enabling source of all that was done.

7. **Titles or claim to fame**. The world loves titles that set people off from the crowd. There are spiritual titles, political titles, educational titles, positional titles, and so forth. However, Jesus said that we are not to seek or claim any titles at all, except to be known as His slaves or servants [Luke 17:10b]. Greatness does not come through a title, but through serving.

8. **Right to judge others and their ministries**. Don't we just love gossip, especially when it is critical about someone else? It brings them down to our level, so we can see them as no better than we are! In this case, perception is everything. This is the way many people look at others or different ministries, "How can I bring them down to the crowd's level so they don't stand out or make me feel bad?" But as a servant, we are on the bottom of the totem pole looking up, so who are we to judge anyone? In fact, Jesus said that if we judge, we are calling down an equal judgment upon ourselves, which is pretty destructive [Matt. 7:1-2]. Our place in life and ministry is to serve others, and judgment is not a form of service. Let's be brutally honest, judgment is a form of condemnation, disapproval, criticism, and denunciation. That's His role, not yours or mine. So let's stick to the key role of serving and leave the judging to Him.

9. **The need to hide or avoid confrontations**. A confrontation in and of itself does not have to be hurtful, because there are healthy confrontations. However, an unhealthy confrontation is a conflict or clash that hurts others whether or not it was intended

to hurt. We live in a world of confrontation, and servants of Christ should not run from them all the time. Sometimes we need to turn and leave a conflict and let Him resolve it in His way and timing. But, many times we need to stand up for the truth in the moral, religious, ethical, legal, political, economic, social, and societal arenas and endure a conflict in order to stop the advancement of evil. Like salt, we are called to preserve good and kill evil [see I John 3:8 where Jesus appeared in order to destroy the works of evil]. Even Paul said that sometimes He allows conflicts "in order that those who are approved may have become evident among you" [I Cor. 11:19]. He speaks of 'approving' one over another, but the Greek word speaks about going into the furnace to be tested and purified <u>before</u> being approved. Confrontations are tough to say the least. They are not especially enjoyable, but the end result is profitable for the whole body of Christ and ultimately the unsaved world. He will commend the one whom stood the test and stood up under the pressure because like Jesus, they will be His best instruments in changing a dying world.

10. **The right to compete or be better than others**. We have an innate desire from birth to be better than others, which should be seen as spiritually healthy when used to develop oneself in a godly way. In fact, healthy competition can help improve us and others under the right circumstances. Then again, there is a huge difference between competition and comparison. Competition looks to excel beyond others, while comparison looks to beat down others in order to look better. Paul wrote that, "we are not bold to…compare ourselves with some of ·those who

commend themselves; but when they measure themselves by themselves, and compare themselves with themselves; they are without understanding" [II Cor. 10:12]. Comparison is for the arrogant and those of little mind or comprehension. The servant of Christ doesn't need to compare, because God has already declared them infinitely valuable; so what more would you need?

11. **Right to reject serving others**. Following on the idea of comparison, sometimes we reject the possibility of serving someone because we perceive that somehow they are beneath us or unworthy of our service. Jesus had no such right because He did not come to be served by anyone [even when He was often served], but He came specifically and purposefully to serve others without exception, exclusion, or apprehension. Likewise, He has chosen us to serve as well, so we do not have the "right" to choose whom we will serve, only to serve those whom He puts in the path of our life.

12. **Right to positions and power**. How often have you thought, "If only I had that position or the power, I would do more for the Lord"? Those in the world seek after positions and power because power comes with position, and every position comes with a measure of power. However, unlike the world, He gives grace instead of raw power, He appoints us to the place where we will be most effective for His kingdom [see Eph. 4:7, 11-16]. Effective power works through purity of heart, and selfish power works through the impurity of selfish motives. For this reason, we should not look for power because there is power through the service that we perform for

others. This power comes from the Holy Spirit who dwells in us. Just as Jesus came to serve, His power came from the anointing of the Holy Spirit, and was exponentially increased as He served others.

13. **Right to determine our marital status.** Nearly everyone wants to marry. This is a natural desire that should be accepted. However, He knows who is best for us, the timing that is best for our life and ministry, and where we should be married. Too often people rush out of high school or college and jump into a marriage because everyone is doing it. Or, they join a church with the main desire of finding "Mr. Right" or "Miss Right". It seems so normal that one should be married by their early 20's, however, this may not be His will. Relatively few believers know their life's goals by the time they are 25, so wouldn't it be better to wait a little so that you can grow deeper spiritually, enlarge your spiritual horizons, and gain valuable experiences in life before committing to a life time relationship? Each person must answer this question for himself or herself because it has enormous implications if it is ignored. Patience is truly a great virtue, and a little patience won't hurt you, but may be the best time investment for your future, your family, and your ministry.

14. **How to spend the resources placed in their control as a steward.** Most of us think about what we can buy, the type of house and car we want to own, and how to use our general resources. However, if we are stewards of His possessions, then we need an "order slip" from Him before we decide how to use our resources. Keep in mind that He has given us wisdom to take care of the general day-to-day

expenses that we have, but when it comes to major expenditures, then we need His counsel first and foremost. Furthermore, tithing continues to be a debated issue for most believers, but, in fact, how someone invests their money tells God a great deal about their priorities and values in life. As stewards, He gives so that we can give back. Hence, we must be wise and careful to provide for others according to His will and priorities.

There are many other things that a servant of Christ will need to consider giving up, but at least you have a beginning list. From here you can build your own personal list of what He would have you give up in order to build yourself up in spirit and truth. Personally, after becoming a Christian in 1978, I began to read through the New Testament with an earnest desire to know Him and His will for my life. As I read through the book of Luke, He spoke clearly to me about selling all I had and giving it to the poor. Because I was so excited about knowing Him better, I began to do that. Over time, this gave me great freedom to move at His bidding, and in 1983 He opened a large door to go to Eastern Europe and live there as a missionary for 12 years. This was not easy or normal at the time, but having given up what would have probably held me back, or at least ham-strung my heart, I was able to pick up and go to Eastern Europe without hesitation or limitation. From this was birthed a large Eastern European ministry that planted scores of Bible schools throughout Eastern Europe as well as in Israel and it still functions today in my absence. So giving up what He asks grants us the freedom to step out of the ordinary into the extraordinary in order to fulfill His will to the fullest so as to affect many others significantly for Christ.

What Servants Do & Don't Do

Servant leaders are called by Jesus to carry out His will. Therefore, there are certain things that we should do as well as not do. The list given in this section is not intended to be a list of do's and don'ts like the Pharisaical rules of old, but is to serve as guidelines for a servant leader. Also, it is not an exhaustive list, but a mere sampling. What this list includes are normal attitudes and actions every servant should display in their life and ministry. Plus, these do's and don'ts should be rooted in our heart and become a natural part of who we are, and should not seem as obligations like a contract. Servant leaders should naturally do certain things and avoid others things because it is pleasing or unpleasing to the Lord.

Doing what pleases the Lord should be a heart-felt expression of our love for Him and His word because the two are really one and the same. Paul speaks about living "in a manner worthy of the Lord, to please Him in all aspects;" we are to "learn what is pleasing to the Lord," and our ambition in life is "to be pleasing to Him" [Col. 1:10; Eph. 5:10; 2 Cor. 5:9]. To please Him means to do what conforms to His will because He is always pleased with that. Just as any good parent is thrilled when their children willingly, joyfully, and wholeheartedly follow their commands, so should servant leaders of Jesus Christ. So, too, Jesus is pleased with us when we seek to know His will, live it out to the best of our abilities, and try to improve our obedience to Him regularly. Here are some of the basic do's and don'ts of a servant of Christ.

What A Servant Loves to Do

A true, obedient, joyful and growing servant of Christ is not perfect, but is one who puts their heart and energies into doing what is best and pleasing to Jesus. A servant leader loves to serve others, even when it may not be the most convenient, comfortable, or desirable thing to do. A servant leader should focus on the positive directives of the Lord, and keep these deeply rooted in their heart as spiritual energizers for their service. Therefore, a servant leader will try to do the following things:

1. **Work for the benefit of their team**: A servant leader is not an isolated individual in the body of Christ, but is an important member whose function is essential to the life of the whole body. Paul says that, "God has placed the members...in the body, just as He desired" [1 Cor. 12:18]. Each of us has a critical part to add to the body which in turn causes the whole body to grow [Eph. 4:16]. If you do not do your part, the body of Christ is weaker and poorer spiritually. But when you do you best, your part is like a vitamin that nourishes the whole body.

2. **Speak the truth in love**: Love and truth are two foundational stones in our Christian existence. Jesus came full of grace and truth [John 1:17], speaking and serving others through it. Likewise, servant leaders must be willing to speak the truth in a loving way in order to advance His agenda and will in all circumstances around us. "Tolerance" has become the call word today, but tolerance that ignores truth is destructive. Therefore, servant leaders must find the right balance between truth and love which requires sensitivity to timing, conduct, and tone.

3. **Share opinions gently**: "A gentle answer turns away wrath" [Prov. 15:1]. Jesus said, "I am gentle and humble in heart" [Matt. 11:29], and He proclaimed that, "Blessed are the gentle, for they shall inherit the earth" [Matt. 5:5]. Gentleness does not mean weakness or ineffectiveness. Biblically, gentleness is the quality of character when servants can control their emotions so as to express themselves in the right way, at the right time, and for the right reason. Gentleness is not arrogant, or aggressive, but it is firm, bold, confident, and calm in the face of life's pressures and the world's attacks.

4. **Guard their thoughts, words, and actions**: Too often we see people who 'wear their feelings on their sleeves.' There is nothing wrong with expressing one's feelings, or thoughts, but the key lies in why and how they are expressed. A true servant leader of Jesus recognizes their lowly position, that they are under His authority, serve as His ambassador for His Kingdom, and consequently need to be careful with whom they share their thoughts, as well as how they act around others, especially non-

Christians. A servant leader likes to be known as a representative of the King, and therefore, will express their words, thoughts and actions in a Christ-like way.

5. **Protect the unity of the body**: There are many causes for division in the body of Christ, and even the Lord allows conflicts to arise sometimes in order to bring out the truth and those who are willing to stand for it [1 Cor. 11:19]. Jesus emphasized the priority of unity between believers when He prayed "that they may all be one" [John 17:21]. Unity does not imply absolute agreement on all things, but it does imply the uniting of our hearts and minds so that even when we disagree, we do not divide.

6. **Think others may have answers too**: A servant leader is but one of many stewards with a calling. Each servant or steward has part of a general outline of what He wants accomplished, but they need others to fill in the blanks in order to maximize His vision through the strengths of everyone's capabilities. This requires humility to be able to say "I don't have all the answers, but together we can do it." I like the acronym for team:

   T –   Together
   E –   Each
   A –   Achieves
   M –   More

7. **Are open to others with differences**: God has created each person with unique talents, abilities, ideas, creativity, and capabilities. The combination is distinctively different in every person, which makes for

a better and more colorful plan. Differences should not divide, but help to sharpen each servant leader by looking at the possibilities from various perspectives. God has created us with many natural differences, and we should see these as opportunities to learn more, as well as to examine our own beliefs and plans.

8. **Allow others to have different ideas**: There will be differences in ideas, especially how we evaluate a situation or try to solve a problem. These are quite real, but tolerance is a divine virtue when employed in a godly way. We are to love people, and we can tolerate them even when their ideas are inconsistent with God's Word, will, and ways. Tolerance doesn't accept everything, but it does make a clear distinction between the person and the idea. We should not get angry at someone else's ideas, no matter how outrageous they may be. We should bear with the person and understand why they accept certain ideas and not others.

9. **Has a passion for ministry**: Servant leaders should naturally love to serve, therefore, they look for people and places to serve. Ministry is much more than an activity, it is the lifeblood of a servant leader. Passion is merely the outward expression of our inner commitment to fulfill our calling to be servant leaders. Godly passion is the release of our spiritual energy when we do what we love.

10. **Divert attention from themselves**: A "servant" leader is someone's servant first and foremost. Therefore, attention should be focused on the "Master" and not the servant who will fade into the

background in the presence of His divine glory. It is true that servant leaders are sometimes in the spotlight, but that is not where they want to be. Like Mother Teresa, they would rather serve unnoticed and, only if He chooses to make them known, then be recognized for their service in His name. Service is first and attention is last.

11. **Serve without prestige or honor**: Servant leaders are not serving or leading in order to get a reward or honor. That should never enter their heart or mind because Satan is the author of such arrogance and pride as seen in the temptations in the desert [Matt. 4:1ff]. Jesus condemned those who sought honor from people when they prayed or gave alms [Matt. 6:2ff]; for Jesus and us, real lasting honor or prestige comes from the Lord and not from man or woman.

12. **Serve without applause**: Everyone needs encouragement to do their work, especially when it is out of the public's eye or the work is arduous. Everyone likes to be noticed for the good that they do for others, but a servant leader keeps his or her heart and mind in check and focused on serving because real joy comes from helping others, not from being noticed. This may sound hard-hearted, but the fact is that we can live without applause. If it comes, give honor to Him who called, motivated and empowered you to serve.

13. **Never ask for recognition**: The weak-hearted will ask for some type of acknowledgment of the good they have done. But a secure servant leader is bathed in the love and grace of Jesus, and really doesn't need recognition. God's word does say to give honor

to those to whom it is due [Romans 12:10 & 13:7]. Honor simply means to show respect or to esteem someone. But a servant leader doesn't look for it, though we may look for those to whom we should give it.

14. **Remains faithful throughout**: Faithfulness can be severely tested under the pressures of family, finances, friends, and foes. But a servant leader accepts the fact that God is responsible to provide for their needs, to protect, and to guide them into the place where they will be the most effective. Faithfulness is a sign of a mature and loving commitment to fulfill one's calling, not in the face of the problems, but in spite of the problems. Our commitment is a gift and privilege given for the benefit and blessing of others.

15. **Keeps a humble heart**: Humility sees who and what we really are. When you think about it, we are just one out of two billion Christians in the world, which makes us just a drop in a barrel of rain. We are not a very big part, but still an important part. Humility allows a servant leader to accept their own weaknesses, vulnerabilities, incompleteness, and need to depend upon others to be whole. Plus, humility sees that there is so much more to learn and understand; once we learn and understand, then we will see that there is still so much more. A never-ending stream of truth to learn to live.

16. **Treat others with respect**: God saw our sinful ways and still loved us. He has a respect for our person because we are created in His image. Even though our sin was awful, evil, and blasphemous, He still

saw into our heart that we had the potential to change, grow, and become what He created us to be. Therefore, we should see beyond the surface of a person's behavior into their inner core, that in spite of their evil will and ways, He can still transform even the worst of mankind. This is a difficult task to say the least, but not impossible. Seeing beyond the actions is necessary because they are temporal. However, the heart of a person can be changed little by little as we treat them with respect. Even the communists of the former Soviet Union were impressed with how believers showed them respect in spite of their brutality. This was a key factor in bringing many of them to salvation before and after the collapse of communism.

17. **Considers others better than themselves**: Paul writes, "Do nothing from selfishness or empty conceit, but with humility of mind let each of you regard one another as more important than himself" [Phil. 2:3]. Paul stresses the significance of regarding others as more prominent, better than, or superior to us. This perspective must be rooted in our spirit so that we will actually treat others properly. The end result is that others are in the driver's seat of our life and service, not our self-centered ambitions, desires, and plans. Each of us is important, but the key to this verse is the idea of looking up to serve others, as a servant would do.

18. **Thinks of others' needs**: You and I have numerous needs, both personal, emotional, spiritual, intellectual, relational, financial, social, and so on. However, the role of a servant and leader is to serve others' needs at least as much as we serve our own

needs. There is an important balance between self and others, and Jesus has given us the way to find and maintain that balance. He came to serve the needs of others and set the example for us for all times, so we should keep our heart, eyes, and ears open to seeing, hearing and sensing others' needs and try our best to meet them.

19. **Willingly sacrifice preferences and privileges**: A sacrifice is a gift of love to others. It is a voluntary gift to help another person in their circumstances. Just as in the Old Testament, a sacrifice was not to be seen as a burden to bear or drudgery, but was a free-will gift to God our Creator, sustainer of our life, lover of our soul, provider and protector. Since He sacrificed so much for us and has shown us how we, too, can do it willingly, we too should do the same for others.

What A Servant Should Not Do

Likewise, this list would not be complete without listing some of the don't's or the negative directives for a servant of the Lord. Remember a servant leader must keep a balance between doing what is right and avoiding what is wrong. Here are some key issues to avoid:

1. **Push their own agenda**: Agendas are necessary to carrying out God's will. They help to keep us focused on what to do and where we are going. However, pushing one's agenda, even when it is the Lord's, can violate a person's conscience by attempting to impose one's will over the will of another. This is neither godly nor edifying. Therefore, a servant

leader will stand up for their God-given agenda, but will not demand that it must be followed or push it through no matter what. Remember that we are just a part of the whole. Sometimes we don't see what He may be doing in others, or He may want us to wait for His time schedule. So keep presenting it, and in His way and time it will come to pass.

2. **Fight for their opinion**: Be bold, be strong, and be outspoken! This is a common belief today, but not necessarily the best way to accomplish God's will for a servant leader. There may be a difference between our opinion and God's truth. When the two line up, we should stand wholeheartedly for it, even if it is against the majority or flow of opinion. However, our opinion may not be worth fighting for, though it may be worth maintaining even in the face of great opposition. But the point is, a servant leader should present his or her opinion with clarity, boldness, and authority for others to hear, see, and consider.

3. **Disrupt or divide**: Jesus prayed that "we might be one" as He and the Father "are" one. Jesus exhibited what "oneness" looked like in its full measure while serving under the Father's authority on earth. We are moving toward that oneness at the present time, though it seems so difficult when so many agendas and personalities get in the way. Therefore, a godly servant leader is not interested in dividing or disrupting God's plans, God's body, or God's will in others. Frankly, a godly servant leader looks at how they can maintain unity with others and how to build better unity for the future. Paul commands us to be "diligent to preserve the unity of the Spirit in the bond of peace." [Eph. 4:3]. He has created us to be

united in peace so that we can show the world that only His people can maintain real unity and peace in the face of problems and everything that normally divides. Furthermore, our peace and unity becomes a witness to the world's disunity and conflict, so one day they will come to His people to obtain what only He can give: true peace and unity. Hence, we press on to build up others in order to bring about lasting unity and peace.

4. **Lobby for our cause against others**: The people of the world love to work against one another and causes that are not their own. Just look at the political advertisement that fills the air waves during election season. Even in the body of Christ, He has given to us different causes, which are led by different leaders. However, different causes do not have to mean conflict. In fact, servant leaders will align themselves with the cause and a leader that flows with his spirit's desires and calling. If Christ has given you a cause, then you will not put others down in order to lift up yourself or your cause because you have something worthwhile to live for. Unless a person is living and operating in clear and known sin, then we should praise and bless others in their labors and causes.

5. **Display anger against those who disagree with us or have another idea**: Anger displays self-centeredness, pride, and arrogance, to say the least. Plus, God oftentimes tests us through how others respond to our ideas. Sometimes we may be way ahead of the crowd, and, when we share a good idea, it infuriates those who want to be first but didn't come up with an idea. It may be that others simply

don't like us, so they are angry anytime we come up with an idea, or it just may be a bad day for some. But whatever the reason is, we need to display control over our emotions, words, and senses so we will properly address the issues and respond to a person in a proper way.

6. **Quit when others don't accept our way or ideas**: This, too, is pride, arrogance, and small-mindedness on our part. When we "expect" others to accept our way or ideas, then we diminish their value and reduce them to a thing instead of seeing and treating them as persons with infinite value. Servant leaders just don't quit; they do get frustrated sometimes because they are "expecting" things to go smoother than they do, but that is just part of the growth process that every servant leader undergoes. Quitting is a sign of immaturity and unfaithfulness. Since He has called us to serve others, let us press into His heart to learn how to remain steadfast in the face of opposition.

7. **Make demands**: There is a world of difference between making demands and making requests. Demands require a positive response on someone's part, whereas a request allows someone to think for themselves, understand, and either accept or reject what is being asked. Never in the New Testament do we make demands on God; in fact, our prayers, for example, are requests for help because we are inferior and dependent. Consequently, when we interact with other servant leaders, we should make requests of them because only God has the right to demand or require anything of us.

8. **Display selfish anger**: When our emotions take control of our spirit and mind, then we can erupt into angry fits of rage or have a temper tantrum. There is a godly anger against sin, Satan, and the world's unrighteousness; otherwise, be careful because it is probably an expression of our will, which is usually rooted in self. A servant leader is on the bottom, so who are we to get angry with anyone? And who are we to point out the "speck" in someone else's eye when we have "planks" blurring our own vision? Servant leaders restrict their anger to godly situations, not God's people.

9. **Express hostility towards others**: Jesus, who was the greatest servant alive, loved even His enemies and showed that love through His words of correction and discipline. He tolerated their arrogance, selfish ways, and all out attacks against Him. But, His hostility was directed against Satan and his colleagues through the power of the Holy Spirit. Hostility pronounces that a state of war exists, and our war is against Satan, the demons, and the works that they perform. A servant leader disciplines their thinking so that they do not confuse the two.

10. **Hide their true and full agenda**: Servant leaders are not sneaky or underhanded, but transparent, open, honest, and truthful. One of the greatest problems in the world and the church today is the dishonest way that many people attempt to get their way fulfilled. Too many Christians are one thing on the surface, and quite a different thing in their heart. This point goes to the motive of every person. Servant believers are to be balanced by being the same in private and public. The saying, "what you

see is what you get," is important to servant leaders. We are what we believe, and if our heart is impure, then we are prone to being sneaky, deceitful, devious, scheming, and conniving. This should not be so for any servant leader, though it has crept into the church unfortunately.

11. **Serve to gain something**: A servant leader should not serve others with the hope or expectation of gaining something, or garnering favor for themselves. Servant leaders should help others with the sole purpose of being God's servant to their needs. Besides, our gain is not in the material world, but in the spiritual realm where we gain more love, power, wisdom, hope, encouragement, and guidance from the Holy Spirit. Servant leaders have already received every spiritual blessing from God, so what could be greater? Nothing, of course. We already have so much to give rather than get.

12. **Try to outdo anyone else**: The spirit of competition is of this world. Jesus has commanded us not to compare ourselves to others, or even compete with others. How can we compete when things are not equal? No one is equal to you, that is, to your person, calling, gifts, talents, abilities or anything at all. Servant leaders should focus on doing, not comparing. For this reason, servant leaders concentrate on doing for others according to the measure of grace God has given to them, not outdoing anyone. Besides, He will judge us according to what He entrusted to us, and not according to how we may measure up to someone else.

13. **Accepts bribes**: Money speaks, and sometimes it

speaks loudly. A servant of Jesus cannot be bribed to do or be anything. Why? We cannot be bought by anything; our attention should be on the Lord and the things of His heart. Bribes are idols of the heart, and if a servant leader has made Jesus their Lord, then a bribe has nothing to hang its hat on in our heart. Servant leaders love to give more than receive.

14. **Put money over ministry**: Every ministry needs money to function, whether it is a church, para-church, or non-profit organization. It is tempting to compromise truth, facts, and character in hopes of gaining an edge in getting support. Slanting any-thing even in the slightest way is dishonest and ungodly. God has called you and me to serve, and He will provide for our every need as we walk along the path of life. Jesus said you can't serve God and money because you will love and serve one while you hate and despise the other. Nothing compares to the value, worth, and person of Jesus Christ, and to lose that relationship just for a momentary financial gain isn't worth it at all.

15. **Care if they become well known**: So many Christian magazines promote ministries and people through their multi-colored ads and conferences. But a servant leader has to ask himself or herself several key questions: Is that what God has called me to do? Is that how the Lord wants to exalt or promote me? Is that what the Holy Spirit is doing today? Is that the most effective way to make disciples? A servant leader doesn't need acclaim, but they do need the Spirit's guidance throughout everyday. Therefore, let each servant leader look to promoting the best known person in all of history, Jesus Christ.

Part II

<u>Servants like Jesus</u>

Jesus taught His disciples to
influence others through their
serving as He did.

Jesus influenced more people in
history than any other servant
leader. You too can practice
His principles.

You Influence Other People

You **are** a person of influence! DO you believe it? Whether you know it or not, your words, actions, and life influence people all around you. This is a fact of life whether you want it to be or not.

But the real question is this: What kind of influence are you wielding? Spiritual influence? Intellectual influence? Emotional influence? Relational influence? Political influence? Financial influence? Moral influence?

Every believer, without exception, influences and impacts other people's lives for good or evil; there is no neutral ground. Your life has power to sway others' plans, to cause them to change their mind, as well as to stop what they are doing and change course. This type of influence takes place everywhere and everyday throughout your lifetime. So take note, you are a person of influence!

One sociologist has studied introverts and extroverts and conservatively estimates that the most introverted person will influence at least 10,000 people in their lifetime. That's nearly one person every other day after childhood. Think about it, 10,000 or more people will pass under your influence, and they in turn will exercise influence over hundreds of thousands of others after you.

One lifetime dedicated to Jesus could touch hundreds of thousands of lives directly and indirectly. Multiply that on a church-wide scale and you can see how one church could literally touch millions of lives directly and indirectly in one generation. In view of that, your life should act like a continual flow of love, truth, and interaction with other peoples' lives.

But let's look at what an average believer's life could do so that you will be encouraged to improve, grow, and go as He leads. Daily interaction on the job, at the grocery store, in the mall, on vacation, in school, and so on will naturally influence between 50,000 and 250,000 people in your lifetime, depending on where you live, work, go to school, and have your extra personal activities. When your life can influence that many people during your lifetime, think of the hundreds of thousands of others who will be influenced by your words, works, and actions indirectly! God will multiply your influence many times over; therefore, take note of what you say, how you work, and what you do around others. Carefully consider how you impact and influence others directly and indirectly for Christ.

Influence is an intangible. You can't touch it, but you can feel it and see how it changes others. Look at Hollywood. The movies they put out influence what people buy, how they dress, how they talk, and so on. The media is one of the most powerful influences in our society today, and you can tell when a movie has exerted influence over other people.

Christmas time is to be joyful, fun, and relaxing. But, it has become one of the most stressful times of the year. Parents frantically try to find the latest toy for their child, or get that special purchase during a "four-hour special" at a store. It is just crazy to say the least. I've been up at 5 AM just to be at a special opening of a store to buy that "super-special" before others get it first. This is nuts, but we can see how children, who have been influenced by their peers and TV, are influencing parents.

But on a more positive note, we know that when a parent pours their lives into their children, you can see their influence directly in how their children act towards adults or authority, how they study, or speak and interact with other children, how they use their free-time. However, on the negative side, you can also see the example of parents who passively or actively neglect their children in order to pursue career goals. I don't say that the parents want to neglect their children, but their career choices sometimes result in this. The children become angry because of the neglect, less self-assured because they faced an adult world with a child's mentality. They will naturally become rebellious by exploring drugs and sex, and are more likely to get into trouble with the law. Every choice we make has direct and indirect influences on people all around us, especially those whom God has placed under our authority like children and employees.

Influence is a healthy reality that God created in the natural order of things. It has existed from the beginning in the garden. Satan influenced Eve, she influenced Adam, and they influenced all of mankind from that day to this. Even though Satan negatively influenced Adam and Eve and undermined God's plan for mankind and the future of the earth, God has sent His Son to redeem us though Christ's sacrifice and resurrection, and has sent the Holy Spirit to apply His redemption to our lives. For every evil influence that has trapped mankind, God has provided a way to stop it in its tracks, reverse its influence, and pour in His positive influence for life.

Christians must actively choose who and what they will allow to influence them: Christ, their friends, their co-workers, the TV, money, or their own desires and passions. Whoever, or whatever, influences you will have an exponential affect upon you and through you. For this reason, it is important for you to carefully examine and discern what you listen to, believe, accept, and think about because these things and people will influence you and others with the same influences that have swayed your life. Sometimes you have to go against the spiritual, moral, and cultural tide of the day to stand with Him. But the end result will be glory, honor, effective influence, and godly change around you.

Key Principle

What you take into your spirit and mind will influence how you think, speak, and act so as to influence others.

You need to know that your personal influence grows exponentially beyond what you see or hear. For example, you influence one person, he or she influences three, and they influence nine, and so on. Look at the "smiley face" which is seen everywhere in the world today. One person came up with the idea that touched others and now touches hundreds of millions daily throughout the world. Or take the example of the "Energizer" bunny on TV; it keeps on going and going and going just as your influence keeps on going and going long after the immediate affect of your words and actions. A person's influence is like a popular movie; it keeps the audiences coming back for more, and spreads its influence from city to city and country to country. In light of this result, it is critically important that we carefully consider our words and actions before we speak or act.

I have learned through life and God's Word how powerful our influence really is. For example, if we criticize someone [whether justly or not] and hurt their feelings, that person will pass on their pain and our negative influence to others. It is like a cancer; it just keeps growing. In 21st century America, independence is a high freedom held by everyone. Today, most people want to do what they want to do, when they want to do it, and how they want to do it. But this principle cannot operate in isolation from others. We live in interdependence and interaction with others; if this were not true, our cities and nation would collapse into the Stone Age once again. Admittedly, we are dependent upon others for our electricity, food, fuel, clothes, job, entertainment, transportation, protection, and so on whether we acknowledge or accept it as a fact of life. This is a simple principle of life.

Key Principle

Our life is intertwined and interactive with others. What we say and do is either a blessing or curse for others. We choose which one it will be.

From the day you were conceived your life has impacted every person around you. Upon conception, you impacted your parents-to-be, doctors, pharmacies, medical staff, researchers, advertisers, the post office, and many others. Once you were born, your impact increased immediately to include more doctors, nurses, hospital staff, your parents, your siblings, your neighbors, family, friends, guests, baby food companies, clothes manufacturers, and on goes the list. This is reality and this is life. You will and must impact others because you and I are dependent upon others, as well as interactive with others.

As you grew up, your impact began to extend to children in your neighborhood, classmates in school, clubs you were in, the church you attended, and beyond. Your influence just kept growing and growing and growing.

Key Principle

Jesus' life and ministry, like the Apostles after Him, continue to influence people throughout the world, in every country, lifestyle, and situation imaginable. As a result, we need to "guard our hearts and minds" because "out of the heart" comes every evil thing "which defiles the man" and everyone they influence [Phil. 4:7; Matt. 15:19 & 21].

Once you entered high school, your impact became more noticeable with other classmates, a special girl or boy, teachers, administrators, cafeteria workers, food suppliers, clothes designers, hair stylists, and others outside of the school. When you began to drive, your impact extended to the division of motor vehicles, the police departments, and court system, especially if you break a law. Currently, your driver's license allows you to impact other drivers [just look at the road-rage problem], gasoline companies, car companies, tire companies, auto parts companies, and designers of cars. One small thing like a driver's license spreads its influences like the tentacles on an octopus. Your life is far more influential than you could ever imagine.

If you got a job out of high school or went off to college, trade school, or graduate school, your potential influence grew as you gained new skills and knowledge. Furthermore, you were influenced by those in positions of authority over you, and you either accepted their influence or reacted against it. Once you settled into a job, you began to impact other employees, potential and actual customers, and whoever you touched in the course of a day's work. In addition, you needed to find a place to live, so your presence in the housing market impacted clerks and shoppers where you shop, home improvement, or the home building industry. And if you have a lawn, you will influence the seed, tree, and flower industry as well.

The list could go on and on and on. You have impacted and influenced people you have already met, are meeting, and will meet in the future. Plus, you will impact hundreds you will never meet. Because your life, marriage, employment, and lifestyle impacts people all around the country and world, you must decide how to answer these key questions:

What kind of impact do I want to have?

What kind of impact have I had?

Do people see Jesus' love and life in me?

Do they see who my God is?

Or, do they see the world's attitudes, actions, and words in me?

Every Christian, young or old, in the West or East, rich or poor, or wherever they are must answer these questions consciously or unconsciously. We cannot change the fact that we have, do, and will influence many people and institutions throughout our life. As a consequence, we must choose what type of "influencer" we want to be. You choose today:

Will you be a positive or negative influence on Christians and non-Christians?

You can't stop it, but you can choose how and to what degree you will influence others.

Let's move on to learn what a New Testament servant should be as well as the biblical principles for living life as a Christ-like servant. God works all things for our good, so even your past mistakes and sins can be turned into positive influences for and through you if you will follow His will and ways in love.

Being A Servant like Jesus

"Servant" is not a very popular term in our culture or any culture for that matter. It has a negative history in our nation, and is a taboo term. In fact, those who were once called servants years ago are now called "domestic technicians" or some similar term. Our culture today has so redefined the term, that the whole concept of being a "biblical servant" like Jesus has been lost, diminishing its impact in our churches and on our society. For this reason, it will be extremely helpful to revive the biblical concept of a servant as defined by Jesus and expanded by Paul.

Defining a servant in New Testament terms is fairly easy. To begin with, Jesus said that He came to "serve and not to be served" [Matt. 20:28]. In His culture, a servant did the dirtiest and most menial jobs. For example, households would dump their waste in the streets, while donkeys and other animals would relieve themselves there as well. When a person traveled by foot, not only did their feet get dusty, but they also picked up the manure and trash scattered everywhere. Once they arrived at a home, and before they would go inside, a "servant" would come out and wash their dirty and smelly feet first. It is at this point that Jesus was willing to define His primary function as that of a servant to everyone around Him. In fact, on the last night of His life He took up the bowl and stooped down to wash the feet of His disciples as a living example of a New Testament servant [John 13:1-17]. This was a dramatic moment caught in time when Jesus modeled "servanthood" for those who would be the builders of the church from the foundation up. "You also ought to wash one another's feet. I gave you an example that you also should do as I did to you. Truly, truly, I say to you, a slave is not greater than his master; neither one who is sent greater than the one who sent him. If you know these things, you are blessed if you do them" [verses 14b-17]. The spiritual and practical lessons to be learned from this text are numerous:

1. Every believer is obligated to serve and "owes" this type of service to others [v. 14].
2. Jesus has given us a pattern to follow throughout our life [v. 15].
3. "You" should serve continually as Jesus did [v. 15].
4. We are like Him, so we should serve like Him [v. 16]. And,
5. Knowing the truth is not enough, we must practice it and we will have His favor and fullness in all circumstances [v. 17].

This is life as defined by Jesus for a believer. A servant leader is fully satisfied because they humbled themselves, imitated Jesus' example, cared for others, and put into practice what they knew. Life is not what we receive or have, but what we do and how we do it.

Furthermore, Paul expanded on Jesus' teaching. He wrote that Jesus "emptied Himself, taking the form of a bond-servant" [Phil 2:7]. Paul and other believers saw that

Jesus had laid aside His divinity, His divine titles, His infinite power, His divine position, His royal prestige, and all His eternal privileges in order to become a "bondservant." In the Greek world, a bondservant or "doulos" was considered the lowest human being in the Jewish world. This type of slave had completed their enslavement to their master in order to pay off any and all debts they owed. Once they had paid their debt, the "doulos," or slave, was free to go and live their own life apart from their master. However, some masters were incredibly kind, compassionate, and loving toward their slaves, and the slave knew that re-entry into society would be very difficult. Also, to leave their master would prove to be a far greater burden than remaining loyal to them for the rest of their natural life. Considering all things, some slaves who were now free, decided to stay with their master and permanently submit themselves to them, remaining part of their household, as well as their property, for the rest of their life. The bondservant now dedicated their entire life and service to their master and all the good they could do to bless the master. If they did this, they gave up all their freedom to become a permanent slave or bondservant. That is, they freely, willingly, and consciously chose to enslave themselves for the rest of their natural life to their master. This was a lifetime commitment that could not be changed because the choice was intentional, calculated, and deliberate. After marriage, it was the most serious choice a slave could make. Jesus, as our example, made the identical choice by becoming a bondservant to His Father in order to serve all of mankind. We too must make the same choice; He has given us all we need for life and godliness so we can become like Him in our life, ministry, home, schools, workplace, communities, or wherever we live. This is the call, the choice, and the position that every servant believer must accept in order to do what He did and even more.

Now to answer the question. Simply defined, a New Testament servant is:

One who willingly yields their life, their rights, their possessions, their talents, their hopes, their failures, their family, future, and all that they are, will be, and have to Jesus in order to serve Him and His will day and night. It is a free-will choice to follow His directions about everything and fulfill His will totally.

This seems impossible! It sounds awesome in a negative way. Who could ever live up to His standard? Not you and certainly not me! But, would He ask of us something that we could not achieve? Is He just playing with us, frustrating our every effort? Not hardly because just "as the father has sent Me, I also send you" [John 20:21]. He emphasizes that "I" am sending you just as, or exactly in the same manner, the Father sent Him. He was not sent alone, but with the fullness of grace and truth in the power of the Holy Spirit. We too can achieve what He achieved, and He promised that we can do what He did, and even more.

A bondservant of Christ generally gives up or surrenders all in order to serve Him and whomever He appoints us to serve today, tomorrow, and every day. In short, a bond-servant only has their time, talents, and willingness to serve "The" Master. But there is a silver lining to this cloud: a New Testament servant has a master who must take care of all of their needs so that they can be the most effective servant possible. WOW! This takes a great load off of you and me. We don't have to worry about tomorrow, our next meal, our bills, and so on. The Master, that is Jesus, now has full responsibility to provide for our food, clothing, housing, transportation, employment, and so forth. As a servant, we are relieved of the responsibility of providing for ourselves so that we can focus our attention and time on the Master's business. It is not always easy being a servant because we have to give up everything. Yet, our doing His will first and foremost overshadows the blessings that He provides for our life and godliness. We can focus on the Master's priorities while the Master worries about the daily provisions of His servants. Now that is a delight to a true servant who understands that they will be far more productive in their life, home, church, workplace, school, or wherever they are.

As Christians, we are to function as servants of our Lord. He is our Master and we are to be His obedient and trusting children [see I Peter 1:14]. Obedience requires submission to the Master's will as well as conformity with it. You cannot confirm to what you do not submit to, and you cannot submit to what you do not want to conform to. Therefore, obedience plays a crucial role in our serving effectively. Yes, you and I will sin and make terrible mistakes in the learning process, but over time, as we put our heart and mind into knowing and doing His will, we will learn and succeed in obeying.

Keep in mind that we are under obligation not only to obey, but also to stand up for His will in every situation. Take the simple example of Christmas and Easter. The world sees Santa Claus and the Easter Bunny as the focal point. When we come face-to-face with those who ask our children and us about Santa and the Easter Bunny, do we shrug our shoulders and say "I want my children to have fun like the other children, too," or do we speak out His truth in love? This is a tough call for many parents, but remember this principle:

Key Principle

A servant of Christ takes what they should say and think about from Christ, not from the culture. If we will faithfully do this, then what we say and do will sow spiritual seeds of life into our children and into those around us when we speak into their lives. Will we bow our hearts and minds to the culture or to Him?

A true servant should never compromise God's principles in any area of their life. But the reality is that each of us has vulnerable pressure points in our lives that cause us to fail, compromise, and make mistakes. Matthew 5:48 says that in the future we will be perfect as He is perfect. And Paul writes, "It is God who is at work in you, both to will and to work for His good pleasure" [Phil. 2:13]. So we are assured that He will bring us to perfection. Therefore, every time we confess our sins, failures, and mistakes to Him and repent, He promises to forgive and cleanse us so that we can start afresh again. We should learn from our sins so that we will not condemn others or ourselves for failing, but grow from them. Jesus has absolved our sins, failures, and mistakes through His blood. Hence, let us focus on doing His will and not on where we missed His will, except to be wiser in the future.

> ## <u>Key Principle</u>
>
> A servant has rights, privileges, and prefer-
> ences. Nevertheless, they are willing to yield
> those in order to serve others through love.
> They do not put themselves first, but second,
> and honor those whom Christ has given
> them to serve.

When it comes to a servant's personal rights and preferences, let us be clear that a servant should never insist on
having those rights or preferences always fulfilled. But if
they do, you can be sure pride is at work. A humble servant
of Christ knows their rights and privileges, yet releases them
with an attitude of thanksgiving and quietness without
grumbling. However, a servant will never compromise truth
or principle, but will stand for His righteous will no matter
what. For that reason, a servant can yield their rights and be
submissive to others at the same time knowing that He is
taking care of them and giving them opportunity in each
moment to serve. A servant serves others out of an attitude
of love for God, received from Him through the Holy Spirit
so that it naturally flows out towards other people, because
service is love in action.

Service – Love in Action

People Jesus Served

Jesus came as a servant to anyone the Father sent Him
to. Growing up as a child in a Jewish culture, He watched

Mary and Joseph perform their daily chores and saw their attitudes about work. In His day, Jesus would have learned carpentry beside Joseph because it was natural for Him to take Joseph's place once he died. But in His 30th year, He knew it was time to leave home, so He was baptized and left His home to serve the lost sheep of Israel.

Jesus encountered various types of people from various religious, economic, social, and ethnic backgrounds. But it all began at the Jordan River on the day of His baptism. Here He saw the lost seeking salvation, the destitute seeking aid, the fearful seeking security, and the foreigners seeking truth. After His baptism and stint in the desert, He began to travel in order to reach a larger audience. His preaching and teaching touched the inquisitive, the religious, the poor, the destitute, the irreligious, the immoral, and others in need. His ministry took on larger dimensions and grew, causing opposition to grow against Him among the Pharisees, scribes, Sadducees, and other hypocritical spiritual leaders. Not only that, the Jewish political leaders, as well as the Roman authorities and soldiers, began to take note.

Yet in the midst of all those friends, foes, curious and non-committed, Jesus reached out to serve them in the way that they needed. When He healed the sick, He served them physically. When He rebuked the scribes and Pharisees, He served them spiritually. When He cast out the demons, preached the good news, raised the dead, or calmed the storm, He served everyone around Him in various ways. His love and service was compassionate, gentle, purposeful, yet uncompromising with its demands on everyone to repent, believe, and serve Him and Him alone [see Matt. 23:13-36]. Jesus' love bathed them with the fullness of His grace and truth, but many rejected it because they were more interested in their power, position, prestige comfort, or possessions. No matter whom He encountered, He chose to serve them in the Father's way, which was not necessarily the way they wanted or desired.

Jesus' life and ministry was full of loving service to everyone everyday. He set the standard that no one could deny. Read a section of the Gospels and ask yourself this simple question: How did Jesus serve the people in that instance? You will be amazed at what you see Jesus did, and why He did it. Jesus' service was intended to draw all people to Him and a saving knowledge of our loving Father. In spite of that, those who turned away from Him had decided to serve an idol of their own making instead. For example, the rich man who had obeyed the law from his youth thought he was serving God. However, Jesus touched the heart of his self-deception, "One thing you lack; go and sell all you possess, and give it to the poor, and you shall have treasure in heaven; and come follow Me" [Mark 10:21]. The rich man was comfortable in his lifestyle and "supposed" obedience to God; he heard the truth that day and decided to continue to bow his heart to the idol of wealth, turning away from Jesus' loving correction, direction, and service to Him. Jesus wanted to save him from his slavery to money, but the rich man decided he would rather serve a false idol than the real God.

Wherever you look throughout the Gospels, Jesus is serving through preaching, healing, correction, and other means. His love envelops His service so that whatever He says or does, it is always an act of service in love for the benefit of anyone who will obey.

People We Serve

Jesus is our example. At no time did He ever exclude anyone from His service, but the twelve tried to exclude various groups at different times. Jesus' service is for everyone; therefore, our service should be too. He came to serve rather than be served; this was His preference. For that reason, we too must choose to serve others as a Christ-like example of our life. Believers should not **expect** others to serve them, but when it happens, we should accept it as a gracious gift from God. Our expectation should be one of serving, giving, and focusing on the needs of others.

Believers are servants and leaders by definition just as Christ was. We should be Christ-like in our serving and Christ-like in our leading. This is not an easy role or task to fulfill, but it is worthy of our very best efforts at all times. Our calling to serve is in a particular order: first we must serve our family, then other believers, relatives, friends, neighbors, co-workers, foreigners, guests, acquaintances, and even those who are actively or passively against us. However, some believers mix up the order to serve others before they serve their family. For example, if your home life is not in order, you may unconsciously put your work-place before family because you find satisfaction and fulfill-ment there instead of in your role at home. For some church workers, they will put ministry ahead of family because they "appear" to be meeting critical needs of members who praise them profusely, while their family only "appears" to use them. This is where a servant-believer's maturity or immaturity shows: do they live by feelings, praise, and acclaims, or do they live by the Spirit, rejoicing and pro-claiming Him? The challenge is great and too many believ-ers lose their way and fall into the enemy's trap, thus undermining their home-life, which actually undermines the church, community, and nation. When the family fails, all else will follow suit in time. This is not God's way or will. Be careful to learn and practice His will and ways.

Our service extends to every realm of life without excep-tion. It is demanding and tiring for those who follow, but rewarding to you and everyone your life will touch. Be warned that you need to carefully protect and care for your health so as not to destroy this temple of His Spirit. If your physical, mental, spiritual, and emotional health is damaged, it will damage all other areas of your life and diminish your effectiveness as well. This is neither God's will nor way.

Christ has created us with an inherent ability and desire to serve; however, we often pervert it into "serving me" instead of serving others. We are saints by calling, but servants by function because saints serve. So often in the New Testament, the great Apostle Paul reminded his friends that he was a servant first and an apostle second [see Romans 1:1; Phil. 1:1; Titus 1:1]. God can always change our function or ministry, but our calling to serve and be servants never changes. It is a steadfast role through which He releases His anointing upon us to the measure that we need it to serve others.

In conclusion, make this definition of a servant your personal prayer and commitment:

I (<u>FILL IN YOUR NAME</u>) willingly and wholeheartedly yield:

> My rights,
> My life,
> My possessions,
> My talents,
> My hopes,
> My failures,
> My family,
> My present, and

My future to Jesus Christ, my Master, in order to serve Him and His will day and night, to follow His directions, and fulfill His plans with whomever He places in the path of my life as long as I live. Amen!

(SIGN AND DATE IT).

Place this in your Bible, tape it on a mirror, and use it as a bookmark. Remind yourself daily that as His servant, your life's calling is to imitate His servant leadership style. May He grant you abundant grace daily to achieve His will.

Serving Through Jesus' Love

We are saints by calling, but servants by function. Our role is to serve others under the anointing of the Holy Spirit through the fullness of His grace and truth in a loving way. The early leaders understood this and did not insist on being called an "apostle," "prophet," "teacher," and by any other title, except in those situations where they were facing false teachers, false prophets, and false apostles. Only then did they have to confront the problem head-on and assert their divinely given authority.

The early apostles were humble and self-denying, using a more common term of self-designation, that is, "servant." Paul introduces the letter to the Romans with, "Paul, a bond-servant of Christ Jesus" [Romans 1:1]. Furthermore, in his arguments with the Corinthians, he wrote, "Let a man regard us in this manner, as servants of Christ" [I Cor. 4:1]. It's interesting that in the midst of a major spiritual battle, he insisted that the believers and leaders of Corinth think of them as lowly servants and not "super apostles" like those who were attempting to overthrow Paul's authority. And later Paul and Timothy introduce themselves as "bond-servants of Christ Jesus" to the Philippians [Phil. 1:1]. Likewise, James, Peter, Jude and John employ the same term, "bond-servant," when introducing their letters as well [Jas. 1:1; 2 Pt. 1:1; Jude 1; Rev. 1:1]. "Bond-servant" summed up the real function, or role, of the first apostles, and it was a term of honor for those who built their ministries and outreaches upon the foundation of Jesus Christ, because He was the "Great Servant" of all, serving through His life and serving through His death. Even in the contentious church at Corinth, Paul could have exercised his authority as their "apostle," but in the face of the many false leaders and misled followers, he emphatically stated to the whole church that they were to "regard us in this manner, **as servants of Christ**" [I Cor. 4:1]. It was a Servant who had brought the gospel to earth, it was a Servant who had died on a cross, it was a Servant who had risen from the dead, and it was a Servant who was the redeemer. So Paul, the servant, was the true leader of the Corinthian church.

In the New Testament, "doulos" was the Greek term for a servant in the church or larger body of Christ. A servant or "doulos" was a common slave in permanent servitude to their master who owned them. Because they were considered property of the master, their life and will were dominated by the master's desires and plans. A servant technically had no will, no property, nothing because all that they were was totally consumed in the master's will. For this reason, when an apostle or leader calls himself a bondservant of the Lord, they are acknowledging that they no longer belong to themselves or to others; they have been freed from the slavery of sin, Satan, and the world. With that part of the transaction completed, they could then freely choose to become and remain a willing servant of Jesus Christ. Interestingly, the Greek word, "latris", which is a servant who has been hired for a task, is never used in the New

Testament for a slave or servant. A "doulos" is not paid or hired, but enslaved; they must follow commands and have no self-will, but the master's will. For New Testament Christians who were either masters or servants, a dose of grace filled this concept with the idea of being godly in either position, and always providing the best for their earthly servant, or their master.

The various Greek words for servant and service in the New Testament draw attention to the whole concept of serving or ministering to the **needs** [that is, not their wants, passions or desires necessarily] of others. Each word elucidates the character and nature of the service rendered as well as the ministry that was to be carried out. Without a doubt, the New Testament emphasizes that each believer should have the heart and mind of a slave so that their actions towards others correspond to Jesus the servant. Having such a heart and mind means to look towards others' needs, serving them just as we would serve ourselves. Even if you are a leader in the Body of Christ, being a servant and serving others is your primary role or function. Naturally, our focus is on functioning as a servant, but the reward of serving others is enormous: hearing more from God, learning more of His will and ways, receiving a greater measure of spiritual blessings [see Eph. 1:3ff], and walking in a life worthy of His calling. For this reason, let each of us focus our heart and mind on how we can serve like Jesus.

Jesus "THE" Servant:

Jesus is the ultimate example of a servant for all believers, as well as the non-Christian world, to see. Jesus fulfilled the saying of Isaiah, "Behold, **My Servant** whom I have chosen, My Beloved in whom My soul is well-pleased" [Matt. 12:18]. In this verse, the Father binds His love to those who are His servants. Therefore, when we serve we can be sure that He is pouring His love into us constantly in order to show love to those whom we are serving. Our serving allows us to experience a natural sense of His love working for us, in us, and through us.

Nevertheless, the Greek word for servant in this text is "pais," which means one who serves as an ambassador of God because they have been chosen, called, appointed, beloved, and sent to serve on their master's behalf. Jesus was the first divine ambassador of the Kingdom of God. He came in the fullness of divine power, grace, and truth, yet without exercising His divine prerogatives. Even though the word "servant" in the Greek is "pais," it is only applied to Jesus in the New Testament. However, it has meaning for you and me today because He resides in us as His representatives in the home, church, community, and world in the same power, grace, and truth. So we are His sent ones or ambassadors.

Furthermore, it is very interesting to note that **being a servant and receiving the anointing of the Spirit are linked together** [Luke 4:18]. If the anointing/power of the Holy Spirit in one's life is linked together with being a servant, then each believer needs to accept the fact that the measure of His Spirit operating in our life and ministry is proportionate to our willingness to be a true servant of God. Service or serving others through the gifts and talents He has granted to us requires His anointing. But as we serve, He releases a growing measure of His Spirit in and through us in order to accomplish a greater measure of His will in and through our life.

Jesus states, in no uncertain terms, His reason for coming to earth: to **serve** and **give** His life for others [Matt. 20:28]. He did not expect to be served because His attention, focus, desires, and plans were outward looking and not inward. The Greek word for "serve" in this verse is "diakoneo," which can be translated servant or deacon. Moreover, it draws attention to the service of caring for someone else's needs, with the emphasis being placed on the practical work performed by the servant for another. This passage emphasizes the work that Jesus came to do, and not the person receiving the benefit of the work or service He performed. So it must be the same for you and me if we are to continue to do His work on earth that He began.

Finally, Philippians 2:5-8 sums up the nature of Jesus' function on earth, that is, do everything with a servant's heart and mind. "Have this **attitude** in yourselves which was also in Christ Jesus, who, although He existed in the form of God, did not regard equality with God a thing to be grasped, but emptied Himself, taking the form of a **bond-servant**, and being made in the likeness of men. And being found in appearance as a man, He humbled Himself by becoming **obedient**…" Jesus took the inner and outer form of a bond-servant, that is, He had the inward attitude and His outward actions corresponded to that of a servant of God. Jesus allowed His human will to be totally consumed by the Father's will so that He always did what the Father expected and wanted of Him. What's more, He served in humility because His attitude was, "I will not assert My divine authority over men." Jesus knew that He would accomplish more for His Father as a humble servant, than lording it over His disciples like the political or religious leaders did in that time. They used their positions and authority to demand submission and obedience from others, irrespective of their calling or character. Jesus' function was that of a servant, always giving of Himself to others so that they could reach their full God-given and God-intended potential.

Believers as Servants:

Believers are called first and foremost to serve. But who are we to serve, anyone? Is there a particular order or priority of serving others? And does someone determine the order and priority? Yes and when we follow His will and ways, great benefits will be reaped for many. We are to serve:

(1) God,
(2) Ourselves, then
(3) Our family, followed by
(4) Other believers, and lastly,
(5) Our neighbors all around us.

This is the biblical order whether we are at work, school, at home, shopping, in our neighborhood, or wherever we may be. Maintaining this order will help to maintain order in our spiritual and family life, as well as in the church which is His body reaching out to the world.

Maintaining the attitude of a servant is not easy, especially in the face of opposition from those who will mock as well as work against us. It is something that every believer has to work at maintaining, particularly when you are tired, depressed, sick, not in a good frame of mind, or simply don't want to serve the people around you. Believers, like most people, enjoy their rights and privileges. But in order to be like Christ, we must be willing to relinquish our rights at the appropriate time for the increased benefit we can bring to others when we wholeheartedly serve them. Whenever our rights or privileges interfere with our serving others, something has to go, either our rights or our serving. If we give up our serving in order to maintain our rights and privileges, then we will neglect those in need, become increasingly insensitive to others, and build a self-centered world around ourselves. But, if we give up our rights and privileges in order to serve others, we will enhance our service and flow in a greater measure of the power, wisdom, and love in the Holy Spirit. As a result, humility should permeate our character so that our actions will naturally flow from Jesus' example of serving without any expectation of being served. Amazingly, when we give up our expectations of receiving service from others, any service rendered to us is a pure and exciting gift from God.

John 12:26 says, "If any one serves Me, let him follow Me; and where I am, there shall My servant also be; if any one serves Me, the Father will honor [i.e., esteem or favor or consider very valuable] him." John places the responsibility square upon you and me: we must continually serve Him or those He places in our daily path. If we do, Jesus promises that we will be in the midst of where He is and the Father will place His honor upon us. This is a great blessing and promise to say the least. But equally important, Jesus uses the imperative "follow Me." This is more than a personal choice because being a Christian and serving go hand-in-hand. Therefore, our continuous service depends upon our continuous choice of following Him who was constantly serving others. Finally, Jesus promises that if we continually serve and follow Him, our Father in heaven will bestow upon us a level of esteem and favor that only He can. Its measure will be out of this world because we obeyed Him. Schematically, it looks like this:

My Responsibility	His Promise to us
1. I continually serve Him in whoever He places in my path	I will always be with Him
2. I continually follow Him in obedience to His commands	I will always be with Him
3. I continually serve Him wherever He places me	My Father will honor or esteem me

Jesus was always in the center of the Father's loving will, and He continually flowed in His power, wisdom, and love towards others, including His archenemies. What a powerful statement from our Lord for you and me! Our obedience places us in the center of His will, power, and action. But more importantly, as we serve in obedience we will be totally surrounded by His love, "You being rooted and grounded in love, may be able to comprehend...what is the breadth and length and height and depth, and to know the love of Christ which surpasses knowledge" [Eph. 3:17-19]. So our service is not so much a job or work as it should be a natural desire to bless and benefit others through loving service. Thus, our service is focused on what we can do for others; and as we serve others, His love will fill us to overflowing so that our very lives overflow in love and service to those we serve. Hence, godly service is simply an ongoing function of a servant of Christ, and we should willingly serve because our service brings life, hope, encouragement, and much more into the world around us.

Servant-believers should understand and acknowledge this simple key principle:

__Key Principle__

Jesus surrounded us with His love even before we knew Him. He has, and continues, to serve us, in and through His love, by meeting our needs. His love for us is absolute, at its highest possible level and cannot be increased. Therefore, believers should be absolutely secure in His love at all times. Otherwise, our service will be diminished because of the uncertainty and insecurity over whether He really loves us or not.

Secure in His love and stable in our desire to please Him, we should look at our service as an ongoing expression of our love towards Him. Yet even when we have done all that Jesus commands us to do, our worth as people is not increased, decreased, or changed in any form or fashion. Our service does not give us brownie points or any special status before His throne. In fact, Jesus said that **we**, meaning all believers everywhere, should say to ourselves that "We are unworthy slaves; we have done only that which we ought to have done" [Luke 17:10]. Unworthy? But I thought that He has raised us up with Him, given us favor, and granted us all of the spiritual blessings of an heir of Christ? Did I miss something? Plus Lord, if we do all that you asked, how can we still be unworthy?

It is too easy to be self-deceived by thinking that He owes us anything for our service on His behalf. The word "unworthy" simply means without usefulness, unprofitable, of little value, or one that has been set aside because they are no longer useful. Why would He want us to believe such a degrading statement about ourselves? This hurts my ego, my self-image, and undermines my self-confidence and security in His love! Frankly, He knows us better than we think, and this truth will keep us humble and totally dependent on Him for our security, to say the least. Yet even with that, we are still infinitely valuable in His eyes because we are His children. Our human tendency is to derive our worth from our work or achievements, or from our family. But from His perspective, our value and rewards come from who we are and where we are. Who are we? Saints as declared by Him. Where are we? We are raised up with Him in the heavenly places now. Consequently, it is all about Him, what He has done for us, what He now declares we are, and where He has placed us in the here and now.

The world's value and rewards may be exciting at times, but they are passing and change with time. Today, others may honor and value you, but what about next week, next year, or in five years? You may be honored at your school, on the job, in your community, and so forth. But that never continues because standards and rules change. You see Jesus does not change, His love does not change, and your value in His eyes does not change. It is better to receive our value and love from Him because He does not and cannot change. In Matthew 25:21 & 23, once we have done all that He will ask of us, He will reward us by saying, "Well done, good and faithful slave." He calls us "good" because our character is good and is seen in our work. In addition, He calls us "faithful" because we were worthy of receiving credit for our trustworthy labors. Friends let it sink deeply into your thinking and spirit that God loves us all the time; He cannot, will and shall not ever change this, no matter what. It is an eternal fact that we should settle into and just accept and enjoy. He loves us because He loves us and nothing is going to change that.

Furthermore, Jesus goes on to instruct His believers in two other key truths: (1) we can become equal in our service to Him and (2) we are His friends. For example, in Matthew 10:24-25 Jesus says, "A disciple is not above his teacher, nor a slave above his master. It is enough for the disciple that he become as his teacher, and the slave as his master." A disciple should "become" **as** the Master which means to be like Him. If our life is secure in His love, undergirded by His truth, we can confidently and boldly step out in service to others. Even if we fail, His love still undergirds our confidence to try, try again. [Cf. John 13:16]. Finally, in John 15:15 Jesus says, "No longer do I call you slaves; for the **slave does not know** what his master is doing; but I have called you friends, for all things that I have heard from My Father I have made known to you." As His friends, He wants us to know what He is doing which corresponds to the earlier statement, "If any one serves Me...where **I** am, there shall My servant also be." Friends communicate with each other, and as Jesus did what He saw the Father doing, we too can know what He is doing and be in the center of His will at any moment to serve others.

In conclusion, Paul tells us that you "are slaves of the one whom you obey," either of sin or righteousness [Rom. 6:16; cf. Verses 17-19]. Our obedience opens up heaven or hell, depending upon whom or what we follow. Since we are Christ's bondservants, our service to Him and His will opens the doors of heaven's infinite provisions as we serve others. What a joy it is to serve others.

Principles of Serving Like Jesus

Serving, in order to be most effective, needs to have clearly defined guidelines. Fortunately, the New Testament is replete with numerous divinely given principles for all servant leaders of Jesus Christ. Without such guidelines, chaos would rule. For example, when you go to a restaurant for a meal, you are seated and someone says to you, "Tonight, your **server** will be _____." But can you imagine what would happen if there were no servers? Even if there were a buffet, we would still have to take care of our own meal, preparing it, serving it, and cleaning up afterwards. So as to avoid such chaos, restaurants have waiters and waitresses so you and I can expect good service, especially when we are paying for it.

But in the body of Christ, or the church at large, do we expect the same? How would it go over with a congregation if someone got up on Sunday morning and announced, "Today, so and so will be serving us the Word of God?" Now that would be novel to say the least! The fact is that we are servants who are called to serve others with the gifts, talents, and ministries He has released into our lives. Therefore, we ought to serve one another in and outside of the church gathering. We ought to serve others as an act of gratitude to Jesus for what He paid to redeem us from sin, Satan, and eternity apart from Him. In short, our service is truly God's design for life and ministry for every believer.

The New Testament has over 30 specific life-giving principles about serving. If you will employ these principles daily, they can change your heart, mind, and life regularly. Servants like this will have a Christ-like impact upon others because they were willing to serve in obedience to His dynamic principles.

Serving God Is #1

At the very beginning of His ministry, Jesus firmly states in response to a temptation by Satan that, "You shall worship the Lord your God, and serve **Him** only" [Matthew 4:10, emphasis added]. The focus of our service is on God, and not a person, no matter whom we may be serving. Why? To put it simply, when serving others we should be conscious of whether or not our service is pleasing to Him. Often Jesus would say, 'If you serve one of these little ones, you are serving Me." So our service to people is actually felt and seen in heaven.

This brings us to the reason or motive for serving. In the church, home, workplace, or wherever we serve, people often have self-centered motives for what they do. They are not so much concerned about how the other person sees our service or is benefited by it, but how it will help them to gain something they want. For example, if I work in a shop and feel insecure because I am ignored, I might work extra hard to show the boss I can work as well as anyone else. My motive is to gain notice and recognition, not necessarily to do my best or produce the best work I can. Now that's self-centered, that is, it satisfies my ego first or meets my needs or desires before meeting my obligation to my employer. However, for a servant, this should never be the case. I should not do something simply to gain approval or recognition from others. My motive should be to work, or play, or whatever in order to "Serve Him only." If what I do benefits others, it will only be because I did it as unto Him. Whenever you and I do our best for Him, it will always bless and benefit others who receive our work.

This is the defining truth that ought to re-enforce our service to others: serving others is the same as serving God! We have a choice, whom will we serve?

1. God –to bless others is to bless Him
2. Myself – to bless me is to focus on everyone else, including Him

A bondservant owes allegiance to their Master, the One who owns and provides for them. Our Master is a good Provider, a good Father, and the One who simply loves us perfectly. Since this is true, then our service should be single-minded and centered on Him rather than a human being. If this is the case, then we will be humble in our service, loving in our attitude, patient in our style, and compassionate in our approach to the one we serve.

Jesus calls special attention to the fact that serving others is actually rendering worship or service and assistance to God because we are doing His work in the earth through our service. Since we are to serve Him first and foremost, our eyes should not be focused primarily on the person we serve in the here and now, but on the task we have set our hands to do for Jesus whom we are serving when we serve others. This may be a hard concept to grasp, but Jesus says "to the extent that you did it to one of these brothers of

Mine, even the least of them, you did it to Me" [Matt. 25:40]. When we touch another believer's life in whatever positive way, because we are the body or extension of Jesus on earth, He is also touching the person(s) through us when we serve them. Likewise, when we touch another believer's life, we are also touching the King of Kings, and Lord of Lords and we have His undivided attention. As a result, our service even impacts heaven. Even now when we serve non-Christians, who are made in the image of God [see James 3:9], we are still pleasing and acceptable to God.

<u>Key Principle</u>

Hate this one ←→ Love that one
or
Hold one ←→ Despise another

In our everyday life, a believer's loyalty, to Christ and His servant principles, is relentlessly tested in the workplace, school, marketplace, on the highway, and just about everywhere we go. Our human nature, at times, wants to lash out at people who insult us, get in our way, take advantage of us or just don't show the love and consideration we expect. It is hard to demonstrate our devotion to God when we are tested time and time again. "No one can serve two masters; for either he will hate the one and love the other, or he will hold to one and despise the other. You cannot serve God and mammon" [Matthew 6:24]. There is no middle ground here; you cannot divide your loyal service between two masters simultaneously! Take for example the following sentence and you fill in the blank:

You cannot serve God and (<u>Money, TV, sports, fear, lust,</u>

or whatever has a grip on you)!
Devotion or division are the two choices we face.

Devotion	Division
1. God	1. God vs. something else
2. Money	2. Money vs. God
3. Power	3. Power vs. God
4. Security	4. Security vs. God
5. Leisure	5. Leisure vs. God

You see the problem, it is either our total and constant devotion to Him [which always includes His will, ways, word, plans, etc.], or division and conflict between Him and us. If a believer serves God and still attempts to serve money or anything else, it becomes a devastating distraction. Why?

Key Principle

To Serve = To Love
Serving = Loving
Service = Worship

Serving is really an expression of love and nothing less than that. We will quickly, wholeheartedly, and faithfully serve the one we love, be it a person or thing, because we see value in whom or what we serve, otherwise we would not waste the time and energy to do it. Yet, you might still say, "I can serve God and other things too." But, His principle is clear:

God wants 100% of your attention, devotion, loyalty and commitment.

Anything less is unacceptable to God!

Now that puts things into a better perspective. You cannot put your full attention on God's word, work, will, or ways if part of your attention is on something else, it's simply impossible. Look at the family life, too many husbands are so focused on their work, they neglect their wives and children, and frankly can't even see the growing rebellion within, which is only a cry from them to "notice me," "love me," and "appreciate me." When this happens, your mind cannot clearly focus on God's thoughts, nor can it concentrate continually on the voice of the Lord; it becomes restless, unfocused, and torn between God's love and what you personally want to gain from your "other" devotion. An unfocused heart and mind is a distraction that diminishes competence, excellence, and creativity in one's work.

Furthermore, trying to serve two masters can take a significant toll on the spirit, mind, emotions, and body, causing restless sleep and draining the person of peace, a sense of well being and joy in life and relationships. Division simply means having two opposite visions. It is destructive to our relationship with God, from which flows all other relationships. If we are not relating to God in a peaceful environment because of our divided attention, then division and chaos will infiltrate our lives, our family, and all other human relationships. Is the cost worth it? No, never! Therefore, undivided devotion to God is not only spiritually wise, it is much richer for the believer and everyone in his/her sphere of influence.

The human heart was created to be wholly devoted to one person at a time. In marriage, divorce is the result of divided devotions, which ultimately leads to the breakdown of the family. This carries its painful results for several generations. Marriage is a covenant agreement that you will be loyal at all times, and will not desire or even think about giving your heart, attention, affections, or loyalty to more than one person at a time. This principle is also true for all other areas of life. For example, investing in the stock market has been very profitable for many people. They saw their investments increase as they put more time into the study of various stocks. Since the result was positive, they naturally began to devote more time, energies, thoughts, and wealth to making more money in the stock market. In 1999 and early 2000, it was easy, fun, and very profitable to do this. But when the market crashed in 2000 and 2001, the investors became fearful, agitated, restless, angry, and so self-centered that they struck out at anyone who dared suggest that they get out of the market. It had become an idol in their life, and that is why Jesus says that we are to serve the living, all wise, all-caring, all-patient, and all-controlling God and nothing else. If our service or devotion is directed to anyone or anything other than Him, we need to destroy that idol and turn back to a living relationship with Him.

> You cannot serve two or more masters.
> But, you can serve one Master well!

God is looking for wholehearted devotion from His children, not partial or part-time devotion. Why? He has created us with the unique ability to give absolute, all-inclusive, total, unreserved, and mindful devotion to one person or one thing at a time. Have you ever tried to do several things at one time? It is very difficult because you can't stay focused on anything; your attention moves back and forth between things and you miss some of the important details. It's like a mother trying to change the diaper on a baby, cook dinner, talk on the phone, and correct the older children all at the same time. Confusion, chaos, and stress galore are all she gets! Now that's not a pretty picture.

So the fact is simple: you serve either God or money. Money is a general term for possessions or things that are found in many and various forms: a big salary, a bank account, a new car, a big home or summer home, a boat, and so on. These things in and of themselves are not evil or immoral. But if our life's energy, time, and thinking are so centered on these things that we are unable to give ourselves fully to Him all of the time, then they rob us of our love, loyalty, commitment, excellence, and steadfastness to God. He is pushed out of first place in our heart and mind in order to make room for something else; consequently, our time, plans, and hard work are now focused on, and devoted to, this idol called mammon. To make matters worse, if someone or something interferes with our "intimacy" with our idol, we get angry and aggressive, usually striking out at whatever is blocking us from our connection with our idol.

Furthermore, a servant must be 'in the know' in order to serve effectively. Jesus used an example to explain how important it is to know Him in order to do the Father's will, which is essential to being a good servant for the Lord. Luke 12:47 says, "And that slave who knew his master's will and did not get ready or act in accord with his will, shall receive many lashes." If God is our #1 priority in life, then we must spend time getting to know Him, to listen to His voice so that we may prepare ourselves for ministry in order to be the most effective. That is why we must serve God through our spirit and mind, and not just through our mind only. If our spirit is devoted to Him, we should then use our mind and whole body in service as an expression of our love and devotion to Him, as well as to glorify Him through whatever we do [Spirit = Romans 1:9 and body = Romans 12:1]. We cannot have a divided spirit and mind because:

> Service in spirit without mind is blind; but
> Service in mind without spirit is heartless.

We must put our heart, mind, and back into our labors

for Him as a good and conscientious servant. A little heart, a little thought, and a lot of work accomplish much for Him.

Herein lies the crux of a problem: maintaining spiritual independence from others and spiritual dependence upon God, while yet serving others as Christ would. Paul aptly stated it this way, "You were bought with a price; do not become slaves of men" [I Cor. 7:23]. We were bought in the past and are continually and totally owned by God forever, not by any person. Therefore, our loyalty is His. Paul commands believers "not" to become slaves of a person. In fact, our only debt to anyone should be to "love one another" [Romans 13:8]. That is the debt of loving service as a servant of Christ.

How can you tell if you are presently "enslaved" to someone, or to Christ? Take this simple test: Can you say yes to one or more of these statement?

(1) You feel hurt when someone actively rejects you, or

(2) You feel more insecure when someone does not acknowledge you in the way you want to be acknowledged, or

(3) You feel insecure around others and would rather be alone, or

(4) You strive to gain approval or attention from others, or

(5) You try to make peace with others at any cost, even when you are right, and so on.

These are just a few of the signs that believers are not living in total dependence upon Him for their security, emotional well being, and sense of significance. A servant believer "knows" deep inside that being rejected by others can be painful, but it doesn't deter them from living for Him, nor does it drive them to seek others' approval or affirmation. Jesus was the most secure, stable, and significant person who ever lived. Why? He lived a life in total dependence upon the Father who called Him "beloved." You and I are "beloved" in the same way Christ was, so we too should be secure and stable, knowing that we are as significant to Him as He was to the Father. Now you and I can live securely and peacefully in this type of relationship!

How does a person become the slave of another man? Slavery was once prominent in the world, but it has diminished to a great degree. Outside of physical slavery, the easiest way to become a slave of another person is through spiritual, mental, emotional, and relational weaknesses in our life. Fear is one of the greatest tools man uses to hold sway over another human being. If I am insecure, unstable mentally or emotionally, or weak spiritually, it would be easy for another person to "capture" me through my weaknesses. This happens everyday in marriages, on jobs, at school, in the government, and so forth. Another good example is when a boss on the job uses fear to keep workers in line; again, this is mere manipulation through intimidation. Politicians also use fear to condemn policies they disapprove of by saying if a certain policy passes, the government will withdraw subsidies from the needy, poor, elderly, and so on. This blinds these constituents so that they will want to re-elect this politician to a position of power in order to keep their subsidies coming. Just take the example of the word "cuts" as used by Washington. If social security is increased by 5% in the first year, but only increased by 4% in the second year, then that has been called a cut. WHAT? Social security increased the second year, but not by as much as in the first year, so that's a cut? What a distortion of truth and facts. But who's concerned about that nowadays? If it works for politicians, then it must be OK, right? For the unthinking, fearful, insecure, and unstable, it hooks them every time and they become enslaved to this type of lie. Also teachers use fear over their students, that if they don't do what they are told to do, the teacher "suggests" that they may fail. It's too bad the Christians aren't deeper and better thinkers than others.

Fear, unfortunately, is a widespread tool of the world. Realizing this, the most frequent statement on Jesus' lips was, 'do not fear man,' whether it be a person, the world, or anything except God. Why was this His most frequent command? Jesus wanted His servants to be "free" from any and all types of fear in order to serve according to His will, and not be pressured by the manipulation of man's desire or wants through the use of the fear factor. Fear can and does control and torment people; it is counter-productive to the Kingdom of God because it comes from the kingdom of darkness, and it is also anti-human. But freedom, on the other hand, releases individuals from any and all forms of bondage in order to fulfill their God-given potential. It will also increase their creativity and develop their ability to serve through love. Freedom is fear's opponent, and will beat it every time "if" we stand fast in His freedom. "It was for freedom that Christ set us free; therefore keep standing firm and do not be subject again to a yoke of slavery" [Gal. 5:1]. God is a God of freedom, a God of goodness, and a God of peace. Hence, a true servant of Christ, who fears God, doesn't have to fear man or man's opinion or what man may think, say, or do. God is in control, so trust Him and keep an attitude of faithful service to others!

Acceptable service and pleasing God go together like a hand in a glove. Paul says that if we serve God and our brother in a righteous, peaceful, and joyful way, then our service "is acceptable to God and approved by men," a double promise [Romans 14:18]. If we show grace, that is, we freely and lovingly serve others without any expectation of praise or reward for our deeds, then God declares that this is "acceptable service" in His sight [Hebrews 12:28]. Can't you just see Him in heaven calling all the angels to look down at you and say, "Now, isn't [he or she] serving others just like I would!" That's exciting to think about. So when our motive is simply to direct our God-given love to others in service, He is pleased and rejoices over us. In fact, "He will exult over you with joy, He will be quiet in His love, He will rejoice over you with shouts of joy" [Zeph. 3:17].

Do You Want to Be Great?

Jesus wants His people to be great, but in a Christ-like way. He encouraged greatness among His apostles when He said, "**Whoever wishes to become great** among you shall be your servant" [Matthew 20:26, emphasis added]. Jesus approves the pursuit of greatness for any believer because greatness is acceptable in God's eyes. However, the way to greatness is not up, but down. Greatness is derived from directing our actions and desires towards serving the needs of others. Examples include helping others overcome character defects in order to develop His character inside, or helping others find their place and function in His body in order to fulfill His will in their life as a servant. There is nothing wrong with your aspiration towards greatness, but how you achieve it is the opposite of how the world would do it. The world engages in self-promotion, self-aggrandizement, and self-protection in order to achieve their idea of greatness. But greatness, from Christ's point of view, requires choosing to serve instead of ruling over or controlling others. As the old saying goes, in Christ's eyes *"you go down to move up towards greatness"*.

Greatness is seen in character, and character is seen in actions. Character comes through personal choices to serve others rather than being served, and it carries the cost of not being recognized for any of the service. Greatness and servanthood should be seen as inter-linked words in the

Christian's mind. Look at it this way:

Greatness  Servanthood

They flow back and forth between each other without one dominating the other. This is marvelous to experience because when you focus on servanthood, greatness is out of focus, but it comes as a natural result of obedience to His will. But, if you focus on greatness, then servanthood will be out of focus, and that is contrary to God's will for you and me.

For example, Jesus said that greatness is seen in the following attitudes:

1. Faithfulness [Matthew 24:45 and Luke 19:17];
2. Sensibility or prudence [Matthew 24:45];
3. Obedience [Luke 1:2];
4. Prayer and fasting [Luke 2:37];
5. And putting others first [Mark 9:35].

How does each of these attitude traits demonstrate greatness? When one or more of the above attitudes is rooted in our every action and desire, then we will naturally do what He defines as great. We will see every opportunity through these attitudes, and this will point to actions of greatness as seen in His eyes, but not necessarily in the world's eyes. One sad example occurred some years ago when a young Christian counselor was trying to help a distraught wife in a bad marriage. The husband thought that the Christian counselor was trying to break up their marriage, so he murdered the counselor without knowing the whole story. The moral of this incident is that serving means giving up our life for others, which may mean death sometimes. Jesus is our example because He was "obedient to the point of death, even death on a cross" [Phil. 2:8]. Thus, godly attitudes are deep-seated beliefs that are expressed in our actions, words and demeanor. In order to change any attitude, the following must occur:

1. Acknowledgment of the present attitude
2. Recognition of why the present attitude is wrong
3. A renunciation of the present attitude
4. Internalization of the new attitude
5. Make a wholehearted commitment to change attitudes
6. Accept that it will take time to move from one attitude to another
7. And work at it until the change becomes complete and natural

When someone has an attitude of greatness, they do not see themselves as bigger than life, or more important than others, nor as first among equals. Biblical greatness sees how small we really are, how totally dependent we are upon God for everything, and that we are unable to accomplish anything great without God's full intervention and support.

Let's look at some specific situations. In this day of unfaithfulness in marriage, politics, and business, biblical faithfulness takes on a more significant character. According to Jesus, faithfulness means devoting oneself to fulfilling the duties we are obligated to perform for others; yet, it also reveals whether someone is worthy of trust and confidence. Jesus tests every believer with expected and unexpected opportunities to fulfill His calling. Sometimes we have a sense of what we should do, or we just naturally do what is before us. If we fulfill those duties, especially the ones that will not be seen or recognized by anyone, then He will call us faithful, trustworthy, and devoted to carrying out His will no matter the circumstances; we continue on till we finish our task. This is a positive character trait that He loves and wants to promote in every believer.

Also, being wise and sensible does not seem to be the most common trait today. Look at the increase in gambling or playing the Lotto. Someone has said that playing the Lotto is for those who are bad at math. Or look at the "irrational exuberance" of the stock market in recent years. Investors were pouring tens of millions of dollars into start-up dot-com companies that were losing millions by the day. The sky seemed to be the limit, then all of a sudden the bubble burst and it finally caught up with these investors in 2001: the market took a nose dive and stayed down. Jesus wants servant believers who can think practically, prudently, and sensibly in their actions and interpersonal relationships. When Paul says that we are to "abstain from sexual immorality" [I Thess. 4:3], that means we are to control our sexual passions until we get married, and even then to continue to control them after we marry. In like manner, John speaks about the lusts of the eye that can entrap us. Credit card companies know we love to spend; just think of those three simple words: "Cash or charge?" Billions of dollars of credit card debt are overwhelming most American households. Why? Because people are not wise or thoughtful, and they're not budgeting to live within their means. Be sensible? Yes! Wise? Yes! This is the way of the true servant-leader.

Obedience is another key trait of a servant leader of Jesus Christ. Luke speaks of believers as "servants of the Word." One can only be obedient to it if they know and fulfill His Word regularly. A true servant of Christ is not satisfied with simply reading the English version of the Bible when they can. No, they want more than a spiritual fix; they want the inner meat of God's truth, the Word of Life. It is their desire to know the depth of truth in His Word, so they studiously search, research, and glean the truths in God's word so that they can "observe all that He commanded"

[Matthew 28:20]. A servant accepts that their time is not their own. Therefore, they must dedicate the necessary time to studying God's Word in order to hear their Master's voice, will, and ways. With all of the biblical resources available in our culture, no one has an excuse that they did not know. He has made His will known, but we must prove it by studying it in detail and living it out daily. Don't expect a Sunday sermon or Wednesday night Bible study to be sufficient. It isn't! Study to show yourself approved is our command; therefore, diligence and devotion to study is essential for a true servant leader.

Greatness also follows practical steps like prayer and fasting. Lastly, greatness always steps aside so that others can be first. Jesus said that, "If any one wants to be first, he shall be last of all **and** servant of all" [Mark 9:35]. This is a pretty unsettling statement: not only to be last and even a servant, but to be last and a servant **of all**. That's the whole point: greatness is moving downward, because when we humble our selves, He will exalt us in unexpected ways to glorify His name.

Servants with an "Attitude"

In today's world, there are many people with an "attitude"! Hollywood stars "have an attitude," politicians have "an attitude," and even rock stars have "an attitude." But is that good or bad? If someone says that about you or me, it usually means that we are arrogant, proud, and independent. However, "an attitude" is essential to life because an attitude is our expression of our beliefs and desires. It determines how we view our experiences, how we relate to other people, how we react to life's situations, and how we plan for the future. Servants, however, must have godly attitudes that permeate all of their beliefs, desires, reactions, and labors. These attitudes must be biblically solid and loving. Our circumstances should never determine our attitude, but God's word must be the source and foundation of every attitude for every situation. Let's look at the key attitudes that servants should possess.

First of all, servants need to be attentive to the world around them. They ought to be "alert" at all times to the spiritual conditions of their environment [see Luke 12:37]. The world we live in has innumerable moral, spiritual, intellectual, and physical dangers that lurk around us. Today, one of the hottest debates is over whether homosexuality is biblical or not, and it is raging both inside and outside the church. Fifty years ago the big debate centered on the biblical position of divorce and the church lost that one by giving in to the world's ways. So today's debate about homosexuality is only the fruit of lost battles that began 50 years ago. Yet, with these and many other spiritual dangers around, we should not fear for our families or ourselves if we walk in His ways. Jesus promises that "greater is He who lives in us than he who is in the world." If we are "in Christ," then He will enable us to meet all dangers without fear or trepidation, but with confidence and humility that He will carry us through victoriously.

Secondly, every believer should know that God has placed a definite calling upon their life as well as instilled a purpose into their life. David, for example, served God's purposes in his generation [Acts 13:36]. Interestingly, the Greek word for "serve" is "hupereteo" which means to serve under the direction of another. David knew he was called as the King, though he was reluctant to serve. After reflecting on God's will and aim for his life, he knew and purposed in his heart to fulfill what God had called him to do, but under His constant guidance, direction and correction. You too, as a servant of Christ, have a very specific call and divine purpose from Him. His call upon your life is for sure, so you should not be concerned about that. However, His specific purpose may be a little less clear. His purpose for your life is consistent with your nature and personality, as well as your desires. For example, you may enjoy working with your hands, so His purpose will certainly include using your hands for painting, plumbing, and so on. Or if you enjoy people immensely, His purpose will definitely include a great deal of people work. It is God's desire that you fulfill your purpose in your life.

Thirdly, a servant needs to maintain a humble attitude towards others. Rather than trying to dictate to or rule over others, they attempt to maintain an unassuming and submissive relationship with others. Why? In God's eyes, no one is beneath us or above us. However, a servant is always looking up and should "regard one another as more important than himself" [Phil. 2:3]. Furthermore, a true servant of Christ will only succeed in their God-given purposes when they submit their mind, will, emotions, plans, possessions, present, and future to Him. Paul said that he had made himself "a slave to all." This was uncoerced from Paul's perspective, because it was a voluntary choice to be available to God to serve others in their cultural settings without imposing his religious beliefs upon anyone [I Cor. 9:19]. But, what did Paul mean when he said that he was a "slave to all"? How could he ever accomplish God's will if he was at the beckoning call of anyone and everyone? Wouldn't slavery to all completely destroy him, or you and me? If I am a slave to all, how can I ever fulfill Christ's or my own desires? It seems that everyone else would be determining my schedule, plans, how to use my possessions, and so forth. Well, not exactly. Being a slave to all is different than being a slave of all. It means to be willing to serve others through the gifts and talents that you already possess; or if you do not have the requisite gifts and talents, you can at least direct them to those who do. Remember, Paul says that "I am free from all men," and to "owe nothing to anyone except to love one another" [I Cor. 9:19 and Romans 13:8]. A servant's obligation is to be ready to serve others, and not to be in bondage to anyone except to serve them like a slave.

Once you and I are successful in doing this, then we can become true servants to others. Paul was an intellectual, a powerful teacher and preacher, as well as an anointed Apostle. Yet, he served others through his various gifts, even to the point of being a tent maker in order not to burden any church financially. Thus, a servant of Christ must be willing to humbly yield and submit themselves in service to others for the greater good of love.

In a similar vein, Paul also states that servants must have an attitude of self-control when it comes to their bodily passions and appetites. "I buffet my body and make it my slave" are Paul's exact words [I Cor. 9:27]. He not only controls his appetites, but he also brings his body and all its passions into subjection to the will of God. Many Christians today serve their body rather than discipline their body, and maybe that is why Americans have gained the title of being the "fattest people in the world." As a little joke, sometimes I tell congregations that we are "temples" of the Holy Spirit, not "cathedrals." In addition, look at the rampant immorality in the church today which has lead to Christians divorcing as often as non-Christians, and some statistics reveal that we do it more often now than non-Christians. What a horror that has become. Now that's a disgrace. Who are we serving, ourselves or God's Word for us as servants? A servant of Christ can and will control their fleshly appetites so that a) their appetites do not control them, b) their appetites do not become a scandal for believers and c) the Spirit of God dwells in them so that they can control their own bodies.

Fifthly, servants are called to be equipped so that they can equip others who will be adequately prepared to serve in a Christ-like way. In Ephesians 4:12, Paul instructs the leaders to equip the saints "**for** the work of service." Servant leaders exist to prepare us for the bigger ministry outside of the church, and it is one of the three primary functions of leaders. In this verse, equip means several things: a) to repair what is broken in a believer, b) to prepare them to launch into ministry, and then c) to actually release them as servants into ministry. "Service" is helping others with their needs, not necessarily their wants or wishes. Service can come in many and varied forms, like helping the elderly with shopping, cleaning or cooking. Or it could be more instructive in counseling new parents on how to raise their child for Christ and so forth. But no matter what it may be, it must have a solid biblical foundation. Even Hebrews 5:12 says that all believers ought to be teachers eventually. However, the primary role of teaching in the church is through the five-fold ministries who are to teach all members so that they can teach others, especially their families and neighbors.

Key Principle

Servants are to equip other servants who in turn will equip even more servants and so forth.

Continuing on now with building the right attitude, servants are to be fair and just with others. "Masters, grant to your slaves justice and fairness," doesn't seem like it applies to everyone, but look at the broader context [Col. 4:1]. A master today can be an employer, a community leader, a parent in the home, or even a child in a club, so it can fit into numerous situations. Fairness is doing what is right and expected according to God's Word. It does not show favoritism to anyone, but applies justice and rules equally to everyone. In other words, how we treat one person should be the same way we treat all people. We shouldn't show favoritism to anyone, especially in the church, workplace, or school where so many others will be affected by what we do. Too often there are cliques in these places, and for servant believers, it destroys our witness of God's justice and love when we show favoritism to anyone.

Second Timothy is Paul's last letter to his understudy, but it is rich with details about serving. In chapter one, verse three, he writes, "I serve with a clear conscience" because what he does, desires, and thinks is right morally, it conforms to God's word and will. Paul is not burdened down with a wounded conscience because of something he did or said, or should have done or said. His actions, desires, words, and thoughts were consistent with God's will and therefore gave him peace and freedom from guilt. This doesn't mean that Paul was free from sinning; it only means that he was void of any conscious evil on his part. Accordingly, servants should have a clear, clean, sincere, and guiltless conscience. What great joy and release this will bring for you as a servant believer. This gives freedom to our spirit to hear and obey as well as that wonderful peace that will permeate your whole being, giving you joy in serving others.

Likewise, in chapter two and verse four, he writes, "No soldier in **active service** entangles himself in the affairs of everyday life, so that he may please the one who enlisted him as a soldier." You say that may be possible for a soldier in the military, but it is impossible for everyday believers like yourself. I have to work a job, keep a home, raise a family, take the children to umpteen practices, pay the bills, correct the children, minister in the church, and so on. So how can a believer not get entangled in everyday affairs? Paul must be mistaken! Not so because God is no fool. He will not ask us to do anything that cannot be achieved as spoken.

Paul is speaking to believers to become actively involved in "vigorous service" for the Lord. On the other side of the coin, Paul is countering the idea of inactive service, which is contrary to our function as a servant believer. For a servant of Christ, it comes down to a personal choice: being in active service for Him wherever we may be, or being inactive for Him and active for myself; there is not a third choice. Entanglement means to intertwine two things inseparably together, to interlock them one with another. In view of that, a servant-soldier never allows the daily grind of everyday life to rap its grip around their heart, mind, soul, times, possessions, plans, and desires. They consciously avoid this trap, and keep a diligent vigil going at all times. This is a hard task to say the least, but if a servant of Christ is going to succeed in serving the Lord completely, they need to do this with their everyday activities. Plus, they should be filled with joy, peace, and excellence, trusting Him to take care of their needs through their jobs, which in turn will allow us to focus on Him, His word, His church, His ministry, and His plans. In other words:

Key Principle

If we take care of God's business, He will take care of ours and more.

So often we think about "tomorrow," but Jesus said, "Do not be **anxious** for your life," and, "Do not be **anxious** for tomorrow; for tomorrow will care for itself. Each day has enough **trouble** of its own" [Matt. 6:25 & 34]. Five times Jesus said, "Do not be anxious," which means don't worry or bother yourself with the things He has already promised to provide for us. Jesus commanded us not to do that, but to continually strive to find and live by His will and character. If we do this, then we can rest and work in peace, joy, and excitement that He will provide for all of our needs. Besides, it is the Master's responsibility to provide anyway just as it is our responsibility to serve anyone.

Finally, true servants must have a gracious attitude expressed in their service toward others. Our attitude in service is rooted in our values and beliefs about ourself and others, that is, what we are doing and how others fit into our life. Romans 14:13 states, "Who are you to judge the servant of another?" Judging and serving are like water and oil, they don't mix and you can't force them to mix.

First of all, God says that we are "His" servants, not someone else's. But secondly, Paul asks us a powerful question, which implies a horrible indictment against all of us if we do judge others! Paul stresses "you," that is **you and me**, should not judge any other person at any time. Why? What if they wrong me? Or what if they have hurt me or others? Or what if...? To judge means (unlike what we usually think it means) to form and express a negative opinion or mind-set about another person that is not sin. Wow! Let's step back a moment and say that again: To judge means to form and express a negative opinion about another person about something that is not sinful. For example, I may talk about someone's weight in a negative way. According to Jesus, this is a judgment because it does not involve sin on the other person's part. Plus, if I speak about actual facts involving someone else, but in a negative or degrading way, this also is a form of judgment, which Jesus prohibits. Now that's a rebuke that touches all of us without exception because we have all formed judgmental opinions about others! But now we know that it is not our position to judge another person's personality, lifestyle, habits, or anything else about them, though we must confront them when actual sin is involved. It is our position to serve others as they are, with their peculiarities, unique personalities, weaknesses, and distinctive styles. It is God's place to judge His servants, and He will remove them from ministry if He decides that they are not fit to serve, as He desires. So the choice is ours, to judge and be judged, or to bless and be blessed. The body of Christ would be a much better place if we obeyed this command and focused on service rather than forming non-essential opinions about each other. It's amazing to me that we focus in on non-essential opinions and refuse to deal with genuine sin. We have it upside down I think.

Serving Others First?

Serving others should be a great delight and joy. Jesus served His family and disciples, the inquisitive pompous leaders, the religious, foreigners, aliens and about anyone He encountered with a need. You are a servant leader, but I want to point out that the leaders in the church should set the standard and example of serving for all other believers to follow. If this is done, then each believer will see and know how to lead at home, in the church, in their communities, workplace, schools, and on the national scene. And His servants will turn this present-day sinful world upside down for Christ.

Jesus said that the leader should be "as the servant" [Luke 22:26]. He compares a leader to the function of serving. Yet, leaders are the ones who are out in front of others, the ones who direct others along the way, yet still functioning as servants in various ways. If every Christian leader were to follow this model, then the church would be a better place, and our outreach to the world would be more effective in God's hands.

On a more practical side, the early church saw what serving was really like. The first apostles did all kinds of serving. For example, the apostles served tables while carrying the major responsibility of preaching, teaching, and praying. However, their serving of tables, an important ministry, took them away from their primary ministry of the Word and prayer. As a result, chaos and divisions began to arise among the believer. So the Holy Spirit inspired a necessary change in the church in order to: 1) release the apostles into a greater measure of ministry, and 2) to allow other believers to come forth to use their gifts and service in practical ways. In Acts 6:1-5, the apostles faced an impossible situation, so they wisely stepped aside to make some key changes. They said enough is enough; find others to take our place because "it is not desirable for us to neglect the Word of God in order to serve tables." The members took heed and selected 7 "servants" to relieve the apostles. Now this was a crisis solved! However, it is worthy to note that the "servants" were chosen for their spiritual qualities, though we can be certain that they were already seen serving in practical ways, though they may not have received any praise or recognition for it up till now. Why was this important? The answer is simple: the "servants" were needed to relieve the apostles of this practical burden in order to bring a greater measure of harmony and spiritual unity to the different ethnic groups.

Additionally, we can "serve" other ministries by supporting them financially. Paul asks the question, "Who at any time serves as a soldier at his own expense?" [I Cor. 9:7]. Of course the answer is no one does. Every believer is a servant in God's kingdom, but for those who serve full-time, they depend upon others to support them in their outreach. For example, a businessman or businesswoman serve in their place of work, but their working also gives them the privilege of serving other believers by giving a portion of their salary to underwrite the ongoing ministry of full-time workers. Servants recognize that they are working in His kingdom, whether it is on the mission field or in an office. Furthermore, they also recognize that their jobs provide them with a salary from which they can give a portion to others who do the work of the ministry for God full-time. This is how the body cares for itself.

Another important attitude is revealed by this question: how do we serve when others are not looking? Now this reveals our true inner self. Who we are is not what we do when others are looking, but what we do when no one else is looking. This is how the real person is revealed. Employers generally have this common concern for all employees in their businesses and workplaces. Are their employees loafing or hard-working when the boss is not there? Are they dedicated to the job or to the pay? Too often workers will strive to serve while their boss is looking, but when the boss is gone or turns away, the employee returns to their lazy attitude and half-hearted efforts. Not so with God's "servant"! Servants are to be faithful and diligent in their work, even when their master or employer is not present, because their service will be judged by God, not man [Eph. 6:5-6; Col. 3:22]. Ask yourself this simple question: if you were the boss and you had an employee like yourself, would you fire or hire that person? If you say I would fire someone like me, then you need an attitude change. A true "servant" of Christ loves to do his or her best on the job, and will do whatever it takes to get a job done well. Furthermore, a "servant" is to render their service in a good and favorable way so that it benefits others who receive the results of their service [Eph. 6:7]. A "servant's" work is performed to benefit others, not just to provide us with a paycheck. For Christians, our reward cannot be measured in dollars, but those dollars are necessary to live in the world. Any job that a servant "must" do or chooses to do is worth doing with excellence. There should be a sense of pride in what we do because one day every "servant" will stand before God's judgment seat to be rewarded for their deeds and the attitudes behind their deeds [Titus 3:8 & 14]. Not only will God reward us in eternity, but even our enemies will glorify God in the present because of our good deeds done to and around them [I Pt. 2:12]. In view of that, we should keep in mind that good work with a bad attitude would defeat the purpose of the service rendered. Also, bad work with a good attitude is no substitute either. The only acceptable standard is good work coupled with a good attitude.

"Servants" need to keep their attitude in line with God's Word while on the job, or anywhere else. But how can a servant do that? Paul gives us a simple answer: a) regard our employer "as worthy of all honor so that the name of God and our doctrine may not be spoken against" and b) "let those who have believers as their masters not be disrespectful to them because they are brethren, but let them serve them all the more, because those who partake of the benefit are believers and beloved. Teach and preach these principles" [I Tim. 6:1b-2]. In short, every employer has inherent value, and we are to treat him or her with dignity, respect, and esteem. Never belittle or undervalue your employer because God has placed us under them for a reason. Remember, if you disrespect the authority over you, one day when you become the authority you must expect your employees to disrespect you too. You reap what you sow. Look at these two commands: "Be obedient to those who are your masters...with fear and trembling, in the sincerity of your heart, as to Christ...doing the will of God from the heart. With good will render service, as to the Lord"; and "Servants, be submissive to your masters with all respect, not only to those who are good and gentle, but also to those who are unreasonable" [Eph. 6:5-7 & I Pt. 2:18]. Even if our employer is a jerk, a coward, or a pompous bigwig, that does not give us the right to show disrespect. God sees them as important, valuable, and worthy of our love. Therefore, Christ in us will empower us to serve and do our job with an attitude of excellence as a servant of Christ ought.

Above and beyond this, a "servant's" service is to be sacrificial so that others may grow in their faith [Phil. 2:12-17]. A sacrifice is not a burden we must bear, but a gift of love that we want to share. If our work is to benefit others, that benefit must reach beyond any financial reward. It must reach into their heart and mind so that they can see our heart and attitude in our work. There's an old saying that goes like this, "Some people wear their heart or emotions on their sleeve." Well, that's true. If a servant of Christ is in love with Jesus, and if the servant wants to demonstrate his or her love for Him, then the results can be seen in his or her work and service. It will shine forth as a badge of love to Jesus. Cooking a great meal is better than cooking a mediocre meal. Painting a room with excellence is better than doing a second-rate job. The evidence of excellence can be seen, and will become a testimony of God at work in you. Therefore, it goes to show that we should inspire people to excellence, not only in their work, home, and communities, but in their relationship with God so that it will spill over into all other relationships and tasks. If others can see that the underlying motivation for our excellence is our love for the Lord God Almighty, it will help them draw closer to Him. Amazing isn't it, our service can be a spiritual motivation for others or even the evangelization of others.

The focal point of a servant's service is to find and meet the needs of others [Phil. 2:25]. Because servants are created to serve, they are "outward' looking." They are looking for opportunities to serve, whether they hear about it, they come across it unexpectedly, or they pursue a known possibility. In a more practical vein, a servant needs to do several things when serving others: (1) recognize what the true need is, not necessarily what the person says is the need, or even wishes for, or wants. For example, I met a drunk on the street one time who asked me for money to buy a bus ticket. That's fine, maybe he needed to get home. So I said, "Let's go together to buy it." "No, no, that's not necessary," was his reply. Well the game was up at that point. So recognize the real need first. (2) Be sensitive to the person's need; empathize and sympathize with them so that they know that you are operating out of your spirit and not your wallet or head. Empathy and sympathy can go a long way to leading a person or a family to Christ and salvation. And, (3) do all you can to meet the need practically. Most people don't want theory, they want practical works that they can see and experience. So keep it simple and practical.

Another key point is that whenever a "true servant" serves, they are to complete or fill up what may be lacking or deficient in the life of the person they serve. Paul said that he risked "his life to complete what was deficient in your service to me" [Phil. 2:30]. People's needs arise because they lack something in spirit, soul, or body. Our task is to find out what it is and fill it up so that no deficiency exists. And just as stated above, it requires sensitivity to His Spirit to "see" what the person's real needs are. If they refuse to let you meet their real need, then you have to let them go and entrust them to Him who is pursuing them.

Finally, God has given many gifts and talents to every believer for a purpose. His purpose is that we may, "employ it in serving one another, as good stewards of the manifold grace of God" [I Pt. 4:10]. The Greek word for "employ" stands for the work performed in our service to others. We are stewards of all that He has entrusted to us, and He has created us to serve others. For that reason, our work should be excellent because (1) it is for the benefit of others, and (2) what we serve out to others we will have served back to us in time. So be careful how you serve, because it will come back on you, sooner or later. Likewise, the Greek word for "stewards" emphasizes the fact that we have a responsibility to serve other people with our gifts and talents. Serving others like Jesus did will keep us focused on blessing and benefiting others spiritually, morally, physically, and in any other godly way.

Practicing Serving
as a Leader

Practicing what we preach lends credibility to our living and serving. Too often we do far less than we can, and get frustrated with ourselves because we know better. Likewise, our doing less than we can diminishes our effectiveness, witness for Christ and desire to grow in knowledge and grace. Today, too many believers are not growing and progressing beyond where they have been for years, which is a sad state of affairs for the church, its witness and the community of faith wherever it is found. So a natural question to ask is this:

<u>How do I progress beyond where I am spiritually so that I can be a better, or even the best servant leader possible?</u>

In order to grow spiritually in servanthood, you need to change your:

1. Your personal value system
2. Root beliefs
3. Underlying attitudes
4. Thinking patterns
5. Response mechanisms, and
6. Living habits

In short, you need a new "paradigm" to live by! A what? A paradigm is a pattern or model that we follow. Hence, you need a new pattern for living in order to become a servant leader like Jesus. Simply put, we are either servant leaders or selfish leaders, there's not much middle ground here. Either we live for ourselves or for others, it's as simple as that. Look at these examples of how our value system and root beliefs affect our view of life:

Present Value System	Revised Value System	Change Needed
1. I'm more important than others	They're as important as I am	See equal value in others
2. My work takes priority in life	Family is more valuable	Work is only a means

Root Beliefs	Revised Root Beliefs	Change Needed
1. I can have all I want in life	I can have what He gives	Trust Him to guide you
2. Money is the way to be happy	Money is a means, not an end	Life is more than money

Our value system greatly affects and controls what we believe about everything, including people. When our value system sees greater worth in the inanimate world of money and possessions, the value of people is naturally diminished. Hence, it is crucial that we learn His value system for all of life so that will believe, think and do exactly as He would. The changes, that become evident as we grow, are easy **if** we are willing to humbly reject what is wrong and build into our life what is godly.

But the big question is this: how exactly do we make a paradigm shift from where we are to what we should be? Good question, and as always, the Bible has answers. Paul's life is an interesting contrast between pre-Christian beliefs, attitudes, and actions and post-Christian beliefs, attitudes, and actions. Before his conversion, he hated the Christians and persecuted them; after his conversion, he loved the Christians and suffered for them. Now that's a major paradigm shift that was accomplished when he met Jesus on the road to Damascus. You and I do not necessarily have to have a "Damascus Road" experience, but we do need to make definite choices that will have the same impact as it did on Paul. But we need to do it before we can enter into a true paradigm shift. Look at these progressive steps towards change:

A true paradigm shift or permanent change requires me to take the following steps:

(1) I need to **know** that a better alternative pattern exists so that I can build it into my life. It seems to me that few believers have taken the time to really investigate the biblical principles, and even less time has been given to study various authors and books on the subject.

(2) I need to know the proper biblical **model or pattern** that my life should conform to. This way, I can compare the right model to my present pattern of my attitudes, actions, and beliefs. It's like renovating a house, you see what you have, but you also see what you want as a final product, and work towards removing the old and replacing it with the new.

(3) I need to humbly, openly, honestly, and voluntarily **acknowledge** that my present pattern is not achieving His will in my life or in my children. This is a key step towards genuine and lasting change. If I don't open up voluntarily, something will force me to admit that I have failed. It is better to do it now than for me to see my grown-up children displaying all the wrong beliefs, attitudes, and actions. It is so sad when we see our children go down the same dead-end paths that lead to destruction. It doesn't have to be that way, so awake, arise and change while it is still time. Hence, we should be free enough in our spirit and mature enough to say, "I really blew it big time." Honesty is an open invitation to the Lord to come in and begin the change process. Once I genuinely and sincerely admit failure, sin, and mistakes, then my spirit and mind will become open to hearing what I need to reject, as well as to accept, into my life for the future.

(4) I need to **admit** that "I" must change some of my root beliefs and attitudes so that my actions will line up with or measure up to Jesus' will. These changes will produce healthy spiritual adjustments in others and me. But the big "I" is what must change, not my circumstances, not my family, not my co-workers, or anything else. It is all up to me: do I want change within or do I want to blame everything and everyone without? Once the choice is made, the results naturally work themselves out.

(5) I need to carefully **examine** my beliefs, attitudes, and actions that are not producing His desired results in me or others, as well as those that grieve others and me. This requires a thinking believer to carefully examine what they really believe, what they think about themselves, and why they do what they do. Paul says, "He who is spiritual [that is, mature] appraises all things" [I Cor. 2:15]. If you are growing in maturity, then examine what is immature in your life, and keep a constant eye on those attitudes, beliefs, and actions in order to bring them under His will and ways.

(6) Then I need to **challenge** my present paradigms that are in conflict with God's model for my life. Now here is the hard part: take a stand against wrong beliefs, attitudes, and actions in my life. The old should be challenged by the new, and the conflict within will produce times of uncertainty and even instability in my spiritual life. But if I keep to it, just like any good athlete that wants to win the gold medal, in time I will see the positive change and development. Be radical in your war against ungodly attitudes, actions, and beliefs. The fruit of wrong beliefs, attitudes, and actions is unhealthy, unrewarding, and counter-productive. A true radical of Christ hates the wrong and diligently works to build in the right beliefs, attitudes, and actions.

> ## **<u>REMEMBER</u>**
>
> Failure is not doing it wrong, but giving up before the changes take root in our spirit, mind, attitude, and actions.

(7) And lastly, **<u>constantly monitor</u>** your beliefs, attitudes, and actions. Old habits die hard, but if you are diligent to listen to yourself, you will catch thoughts, ideas, yearnings, words, and actions that are contrary to the changes you want to make. So when you are wrong, correct the wrong ones, then take the time to retrain and reeducate yourself by regularly building His truth into your thought life and spirit. Over time, you will begin to develop godly beliefs, attitudes, and actions, which will become natural to you.

In order to make the paradigm shift and bring about permanent change, something must trigger a desire in us for change. God must be able to bring His thoughts, desires, and will into ours so that we can employ His principles and vision in our life and ministry. Consequently, we must seek to instill godly values as the foundation of our daily life, godly principles as our operating values, and godly vision as the goal that we are reaching towards. If we do this, then will maximize our growth and change for Christ.

If we have His goal, then we can see His vision for our life; if we have His principles, then we can live His truth everyday; and if we have His values, then we choose to do what is always right. Picture it this way:

3. Goal: God's Vision Point Us Forward

2. God's Principles: ➞ ⬆ ⬆ ⬆
Permeate Our Living

1. Foundation: God's Values Fill Our Life

This is a tall order that requires a great deal of time, energy and effort on your part. However, the reality is if you really want to make the necessary changes, then (1) you will commit the necessary time, energy, and effort. (2) You will fail at times, but don't quit even when you "feel" that none of your effort is paying off. Patience is the greatest virtue here. (3) You will mistakenly think that no matter how much effort you put into changing, you will never be able to achieve lastly change. And, (4) keep in mind that quitters never win and winners never quit, though they may want to and think about a 1,000 times. Even when they are the most frustrated and angry with themselves, they recognize that perseverance is the key to achieving the goal of change. Jesus taught His disciples about paradigm shifts all the time, and below is a sample schematic that highlights some of the pattern changes that need to be implemented in our life so that we can be the greatest servant leaders possible.

You can change and **you will** change "**if**" you want to change. When you put your heart into change, you will experience His Word, will, promise, and power working greatly in you towards perfection. However, change requires revealing what is wrong, removing it, and then refreshing yourself through His truth. Look at how the change must be done:

Moving from the old paradigm to the new paradigm

Old Paradigm	Change Needed	New Paradigm
1. Leaders must dictate	Others can lead too	Leaders must trust others
2. Leaders never affirm others	Serve others in love	Leaders affirm & encourage
3. Leaders are on top	Top is at the bottom	Leaders serve all others
4. Love has no place in leadership	Leaders care for others	Love others like yourself
5. Leaders are served by others	Leaders expect to serve	Leaders serve others first
6. Leaders love those who help them	Love is due to to everyone	Leaders can serve in love
7. Leaders focus on the results	Leaders focus on people	Leaders see people, then results

This schematic list could go on and on. But the picture is clear: today's leaders, whether in the home, church, schools, workplaces, government, or communities, must see the need for a new paradigm in their beliefs, attitudes, and actions. Only when these have been changed to conform to His will, will we be able to fulfill Christ's will to "serve" others effectively.

Servant leadership is a unique paradox for many people, including Christians. Being a servant and a leader simultaneously appear to be at odds with one another. In reality, this is not so for Christians, though it is definitely in conflict with the non-Christian culture around us. That culture proclaims that leaders do not serve others because they rule by controlling, dominating or using subtle power-games in order to gain the advantage to get to the top. In contrast, the Christian perspective of being a servant and leader should not be seen as either a paradox or a conflict with one another. In fact, servant leadership is simply two sides of the same coin, only emphasizing a different function depending on which side you are looking at. Servant leadership is both biblical and essential to our personal transformation, as well as that of our homes, schools, workplaces, churches, communities, and nations.

Change does not come easily for most people, so it must be implemented over time. One of the key factors in achieving any type of change is practice. Regular practice will bring lasting results because it changes the root beliefs and attitudes that come forth in our actions. Paul was a great apostle, teacher, preacher, and author, but he had to practice his new beliefs, attitudes and actions continually in order to constantly walk in the Spirit. Not only did he have the right theory, but he demonstrated his spiritual beliefs and values in practical ways also by ministering to the material needs of other believers [Rm. 15:25]. He put his money where his heart and mouth were.

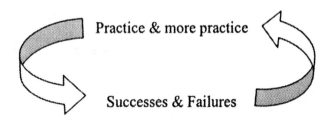

This is an endless cycle. You practice your principles, you succeed and fail, but you keep on practicing so you succeed some of the time and fail some of the time. The cycle continues, but the internal and external changes in your life proceed upward, even if it is ever so gradual. It's like driving up a slow incline that has many bumps and potholes along the way; it's rough at times, but it gets you to the top. This is the way it will be for you and me when we practice His principles in our life so that they become our principles, our beliefs, our attitudes, and our actions.

Remember the old proverb that says, "practice makes perfect"? It will work for anyone if they will diligently practice any biblical principle until they perfect it. Whatever you may be attempting to change in your life, He guarantees that He "is at work in you, both to will and to do His good pleasure." Furthermore, "He who began a good work in you will perfect it," and if we endure by practicing, we will "be made perfect and complete, lacking in nothing" [Phil 2:13; 1:6; Jas. 1:4]. Take for example the question of giving or tithing? The average person gives about 2% of their income to all charities. Few actually practice tithing, so how can you or I make it a normal part of our life? If you give various amounts now and then, it will be hard to develop a joyful practice of giving regularly; and if you give large sums now and then, it will also be hard to develop the practice of giving systematically. Look at the contrast that believers face: statistics show us that Christians on average give 3% to 5% of their income to church, but spend tens of billions of dollars on cosmetics, vacations, leisure, pet care, and so forth. The natural question to ask is this: what belief system is demonstrated here? Simple, my external comfort, appearance, and agenda are more important than His eternal kingdom. We could say that we practice giving to our own desires and needs, so why not try to practice giving to His desires and needs? If you are willing to begin the regular practice of tithing, over time it will become more natural, eventually becoming a part of your mindset and character. Where the treasure is, there will be your heart in action also.

Let's carry this principle further into other areas of our life. There is no question that a natural tension exists between our need for security and the insecurity that crops up in all of us about giving. Some will think, if I give too much, then how will I live and pay all my bills? Will I be able to have a vacation? What about my children, or what about me being able to afford a home? Too often our trust is more in our abilities to make a living and what we see, rather than who our Master is and what He promises to provide. A true servant of Jesus has a different attitude about money. God is our Master, our source of life, our provider, our protector and Father who cares for us completely and perfectly. We are totally dependent upon Him for all things in life, so why not trust Him first and foremost? If we obey what He asks, He will provide for all of our needs. Now that's a security you can bank on. Trusting Him because He trusts us to do what He asks. In fact, Paul says that giving is considered an important form of spiritual service [2 Cor. 9:12]. Practicing a simple thing like tithing and giving are seen by God as a form of spiritual service by His servants. What freedom there is within us when we follow His will; it produces a natural excitement and expectation that He will meet our needs. No problems, no worries, and no concern for those who trust Him always! He is there for us and will provide for us.

Another example of how we can practice our serving is to open our home for His work to such things as Bible studies and so forth [Rm. 16:1-2]. Our home is a place of refuge not only for ourselves, but it can be, also, for others as well. We should open our homes to welcome friends, neighbors, and unexpected visitors, as well as anyone who may come in need. Every visitor gives us an opportunity to serve them in practical ways, and hopefully opens the door to instruct them in His ways. Instructing others is a key form of service as Paul points out to Timothy that, "In pointing out these things…[that's is, the false doctrines] you will be a good servant of Christ." Paul wants him to be "constantly nourished on the words of the faith and of the sound doctrine which you have been following" so that he can in turn serve others through his faith and sound doctrine [I Tim. 4:6]. In many ways this is very similar to Hebrews 5:12, which says, "For though by this time **you** ought to be teachers." The writer makes it clear that every believer should be able to teach basic truth to anyone, which is one of the greatest forms of serving another by feeding him or her the truth.

Unique Perspective of Servants

In bringing this section to a conclusion, it will be helpful to see life from a servant's perspective in order to see what advantage is gained from it. Servants have an opportunity to see life, and in particular, people in a far clearer way than most may realize. First of all, since a servant is considered to be at the bottom scale of life, everything and everyone is above them, so they see people and life by looking up. Secondly, servants are not considered worthy, important, or of any particular value. Consequently, most people act and react in their presence without any inhibitions or hidden agenda around them. Thirdly, servants are generally treated without consideration for who they are or know, or for what they think or believe, or for what they might say to others about what they have observed or heard from the "upper" class. And fourthly, servants are usually dismissed because they are "seen" as relatively ignorant, or unable to comprehend what others may be saying, doing or planning. As a result, people do not try to garner a servant's favor, nor do they attempt to treat them with deference or respect. Nor do they endeavor to appear good in their eyes, because servants are of no value anyway.

As a natural consequence, a servant will see people for who and what they really are, as well as what life is really about. From a servant's perspective, they get to see into the hearts and lives of other people through the way they treat others, and how they may treat or mistreat them by their words, subtle attitudes, and actions. Servants see and experience people's inner beliefs and attitudes in their behavior because their treatment really reveals what they think about them. Thus, servants appear to have no position, power, or prestige to protect, and for that reason, they receive uncolored treatment from others around them, and see the world from the bottom up.

However, a true servant of Christ really has great power because of the high spiritual position they occupy. Jesus said that we have been "**raised up** with Him **and seated** us with Him in the heavenly places, in Christ Jesus" [Eph. 2:6]. Spiritually we occupy a position of heavenly power, but the interesting thing is that our power comes from serving others. Even though our position comes from Christ who is seated at the right hand of the Father now, we are not to use that position for selfish reasons, but as a blessing to others. Servant leaders are unique people in the world, so let us seek to serve others in order that we might lead them to salvation and genuine Christian living, so that they too can become change-agents in their communities and nations.

A Servant is...

It is always good to see in a concise way what a servant really is. It helps to quickly review what you are to be so that you can pray each of these statements as a prayer of commitment to Jesus Christ. Listed below are a few statements of what a servant is, but you should add to it and make it a very personal prayer for your life and ministry. A servant is...

Always under His authority, at all times in all places...

One who seeks to imitate the greatest Servant of all, Jesus...

One who recognizes that serving must come from the heart...

Based on love for Jesus and others...

One who wants to help others become the best them can...

One who doesn't expect to receive much...

One who wants to give much...

The person who gives up their rights and accepts wrongs as normal...

A person whose life is dedicated to serving others...

One who is a steward of all they have...

One who sees service before anything else...

One who accepts their lowly position as a mark of greatness...

One who doesn't complain but compliments...

Dedicated to building others up in grace...

Quick to think about what He wants first...

One who seeks to build unity and maintain it...

Committed to influencing others positively for Christ...

One who loves serving instead of commanding...

Devoted to impacting his/her home, church, community and nation for Christ.

Part III
<u>Leading like Jesus</u>

Jesus came to lead all people out of sin and the control of the kingdom of darkness, into a living and loving relationship with almighty God. We too are called to do the same thing, to lead in a way that shows His love and compassion.

You Are a Leader

Y ou are a leader! God has created you to lead others, and now is the time to learn all of the principles of Jesus-like leadership. "George Barna, the famous Christian researcher, writes on his web site that, '63% of Americans feel they are seen as a leader by other people. This is merely a confirmation of God's word that all believers are already leaders." No matter where you are in your life, you are gifted as a leader of one or more people around you. Leaders make choices and decisions just as you do everyday. Therefore, be diligent in your preparations, because your life will impact many others for good or evil. It is His will that your life positively blesses and impacts others with truth and grace for years to come.

New Testament believers are called to be servants who lead in life. You might ask yourself, "Is this another paradox to understand?" No, not at all. It is a fact that those who serve the most will lead the most. Likewise, those who lead the most will also serve the most. Jesus came to serve and lead simultaneously as a living example for you and me. The more He led the more He served, and vice versa. His service led to ministry and His leading led to service. In His travels, He encountered many types of people and problems, but no matter what, He served them by leading them to the truth, though some preferred not to accept it. When He healed a bodily sickness, the truth was that God loves to restore a sickly body to health. When He encountered the Pharisees, the truth was that they, as appointed spiritual leaders, were defrauding the people of God's truth. When He met a demon-possessed person, the truth was that He was redeeming mankind from the hold of darkness and restoring them to a living relationship just as Adam and Eve had in the garden. So truth overcame every obstacle He faced, and restored life to those who would receive it.

Towards the end of His earthly ministry, He said to His disciples that "I send you just as My Father sent Me," that is, to serve and lead in the anointing and power of His truth and Spirit. They were to be as equipped as Jesus was so as to face the world around them without fear, but with boldness, confidence, and assurance that they would overcome.

Today, as well as everyday, we are called upon to serve and lead others just as Jesus did. Whether we do it as a parent in a family, a child with their peers, a husband as head of his wife, an employee at work, an elder or deacon in the local church, a community leader, politician, or whatever position a believer may hold, we are to serve and lead like Him. The New Testament makes it very clear that we are called, gifted, and anointed to lead by serving others. This is a joy to fulfill His calling upon our life, and to be the quality servant leaders He wants.

> # Serve by leading
> # and
> # Lead by serving
>
> Serving and leading are intricately linked in every believer, whether we do it for Christ or ourselves.

Keep in mind that we are not anointed to be able to give demonstrations of power through signs and wonders. No, we are anointed in order to serve others through and with that anointing. When Jesus was faced with the temptation to show His power, He refused to do it because it would not serve the Father's purposes. Therefore, we need to be careful not to flaunt our anointing or spiritual gifts, but to humbly employ them for the loving benefit of others. But when we do that, the release of God's power through us is a sign that He is with us, is using us, and wants to help others come into a living relationship with Him. Power is wonderful, but it must be controlled by the overriding plans that He has for it: to reveal His presence and ability to change lives and destinies.

Jesus as **THE** Leader:

Jesus was the master leader 'par excellence.' He demonstrated what it meant to lead people out of darkness into the light, out of evil into righteousness, out of the kingdom of Satan into the Kingdom of God, out of fellowship with sin into fellowship with the Creator, and out of bondage into eternal freedom through salvation.

Jesus came to establish a New Kingdom and a new way of life by turning the world upside down. In Jesus' situation, serving was His calling and leading was His function, or the result of His calling. Therefore, Jesus set the stage for all future believers to be anointed to serve whomever we encounter, and gifted to lead whomever will follow.

We note that Jesus served everyone He encountered, whether they came with selfish motives or godly motives. Many of those who desired physical healing did not have faith, but He healed them because He came to serve first and foremost. Likewise, whenever and wherever He served, He used that opportunity to lead everyone to the Truth, the revelation of God, and the living Word of God, Himself. So Jesus' life was consumed with serving and leading from beginning to end.

<u>Believers are Leaders</u>:

Every believer on earth, whether they are young or old, rich or poor, from the East or West, or wherever they may be, is called to be a leader of both individuals, families, communities, and nations. This seems like a tall task, but in reality it is what He has sent us to do in His absence. We are "in" the world in order to make a difference of the world. Therefore, there are no limits whom we may serve and lead. Look at these modern day examples:

1. Christian children can lead other children;
2. Christian parents should naturally lead their children;
3. A Christian husband can lead His wife, whether she is a Christian or not;
4. Elders are anointed to lead the members of a local church;
5. Believers are to lead in their workplace;
6. Christians should lead by setting the direction of the cities, states and nations;

7. And every believer can lead their neighbors no matter where they are.

It is imperative for every Christian to see that they have spiritual, moral, personal, intellectual, and inter-relational influence with and over many people. Influence is an intangible that goes far beyond any immediate contact, and Christians should take advantage of influencing others near and far. Much of a believer's influence is indirect, rather than direct, but it is still influence. For example, a parent influences their child concerning TV programs, and the child will influence their friends who in turn will influence their parents and so on.

Parent ➔ their child ➔ a friend ➔ friend's parent

Two-third's of a parent's influence is indirect, but it touches many more people than they may anticipate or even realize. Therefore, believers have a much greater God-given influence on others than ever imagined, be it negative or positive. Christians should take hold of this principle and let His Spirit work through them to influence their community, work-place, schools, neighborhoods, and beyond for the good of advancing His kingdom principles in this world. It is incumbent that all believers, because they have positions of authority, recognize that their words, attitudes, actions, and behavior will have a considerable influence far beyond the present time, but will carry on even beyond their lifetime. Take for example the hurtful words of a parent to their child. When a parent belittles and ostracizes a child, especially in the presence of their peers, that pain, if not healed, will carry on long after the parent has died. This is the way influence can carry on for years after one's death. So like Jesus, let our influence be for godliness and godly change.

Carrying this principle further, let's look at day-to-day

reality: (1) Christian children spend time with their peers everyday. They can have a dramatic influence upon their generation and several to come by their words, actions, and refusals to go along with the crowd. It will take courage to do this, but the results will be phenomenal. They can serve their peers in various ways and simultaneously lead them to Christ and a Christ-like lifestyle. (2) Christian parents can serve their children in various ways by leading them first into a living relationship with Christ so that they will live a godly life that influences others for good. If parents can do this, their children will have a positive influence upon the generation to come. (3) Elders should serve their congregations by leading them into a vital relationship with His word, so that their lives are examined under the microscope of His truth that will lead them to change what needs to be changed in such a way that they become change-agents for others. (4) Churches and/or Christian families/individuals can serve their communities in very practical ways like cleaning up their neighborhoods in order to beautify their surroundings, which will give them opportunity to lead their neighbors to the Truth. And finally, (5) Christians, whom God has placed in key positions of influence, can serve others as well. God has placed some in the government, over education, in the legal system, arts and entertainment, business community, etc., to serve people all around them by focusing on their needs in order to lead them to the One who has the answers to all the questions and problems. Thus, many believers regularly function as leaders in many and various ways without ever having chosen to be leaders. They can and should bring blessings and benefits to countless people in their spheres of influence.

Christians, by nature, are leaders because Jesus has placed them in positions of great influence starting in the home and leading all the way up to the White House. He says that we have been raised up with Him already, so spiritually we sit in heavenly places with heavenly influence in the earth that must be exercised in accordance with His will [Eph. 2:6]. Accordingly, our approach to leadership is significantly different from the world's approach. Christians are called to be servant leaders that do not look for the power, position, or prestige, but for opportunities to serve where they are and when they can, as examples of Christ. Believers should seek to serve humbly and lovingly, allowing God to exalt them if He so chooses in the right way and at the right time, in order to maximize their spiritual influence with others to bring about godly transformation. Finally, believers should recognize and accept that every time we serve someone, we are ministering in His name. Take the example of a nurse that serves on the maternity ward. Just praying quietly over the newborns can be the beginning of a godly start for those who may not even have Christian parents. So our opportunities are limitless, and God has placed us where we need to be in order to serve and lead others.

Key Foundational Principle of this study

All believers should meet the qualifications of a leader no matter what their position is in the home, church, workplace, school, community, or nation because they may be called upon at any time to lead others. Hence, they must be qualified before they are called. For example, an elder does not suddenly develop the qualities of an elder after becoming an elder, but will have naturally exhibited those qualifies long before they are called and recognized. Consequently, future leaders are already leading others in small ways, and they are doing it long before they are chosen to lead in a more public position.

This is especially true for the family. A leader in the family will exhibit leadership qualities while leading and serving their family, relatives, and neighbors long before they have been recognized outside of the family and community. The family must first recognize, accept, and yield to their leadership before any others will accept and yield as well. If they cannot lead their family, they cannot lead others.

A Leader Who Serves

Who is a leader, and what is a leader? It will be helpful to define what is a leader for the reader. A **leader** is one who has the following characteristics:

1. A living relationship with the Father through Christ;
2. An active obedience to His will;
3. A readiness to change and grow mature spiritually;
4. An anointing from the Holy Spirit;
5. God-given talents and abilities;
6. A natural willingness to step out and serve others;
7. And takes practical steps to fulfill their calling by meeting the needs of others.

Each of these characteristics is essential to a servant leader. They are intimately linked together in order to form a perfect servant leader. Together these seven fill a servant leader with the necessary requisites for serving in the same spirit and way Jesus did. Jesus walked in each of these seven, as well, and impacted the Jewish world around Him. Today we live in a world in desperate need of God's love and redemption. Those who will serve others will become the leaders of the next generation. Just look at our public school system; it is in complete shambles. Violence rules, academic scores are at the lowest levels in decades, morals are all but non-existent, and there is little or no hope for improvement in the future. Where are the servant leaders? We are those who can take a bad situation and transform it. It has been done before since the creation of the church, and it will be done again, and again and again. You and I have to take our role and responsibility very seriously if we are going to impact our world like Jesus did.

A true leader knows that their talents and abilities are a pure gift from God to bless and enrich others. But to enrich others, we have to know that they are poor because we don't want to enrich those who may already be rich spiritually. He has released these talents and abilities into us as good stewards. Therefore, we are to use them to:

a) equip by repairing the brokenness in others;
b) train others through His truth that will captivate their hearts and minds by making them servant leaders of Christ, too;
c) empower them to overcome evil with His good;
d) guide them in their everyday life as well as life's decisions that came their way;
e) develop them into the full person with the full potential that He has given to each and every person;
f) heal them of all their hurts and wounds, whether

they be self-inflicted or other-inflicted; and

g) release them into life and service so that they too can lead as servants in their home, church, community or nation as well.

This is the multiplying affect of servant leadership. A leader intentionally and purposefully serves others so that they can fulfill their God-given role and responsibility as a part the body of Christ living and ministering in the world. Whenever a servant leader uses their gifts and talents, God continues to release more and more of their potential for the benefit of others. The result of this will be that others will naturally and readily follow those who serve them just as many followed Jesus and the Apostles after Him.

It is truly a great joy and privilege to be a leader who serves. Jesus has set a rather challenging example before us, and with so many scandals in recent years among evangelical and charismatic leaders, it is sometimes hard to find living models that we can imitate. However, this is where our determination and desires come into play: we can do it ourselves if we so choose. Models are great to have, as is encouragement from others, but even without them we can still achieve His goals in our life. It takes a determined soul to follow His will, and you or I can do it. As the proverb goes, "Whatever you set your mind to do you can do."

It is too easy to lead without serving, or to lead with an attitude of dominance over others. Jesus said that we are to lead as servants, that is, with a servant's heart, attitude, and actions. Therefore, let us incorporate the seven essential characteristics listed above into our daily lives.

Leading Through Jesus' Love

L ove is the root of the spiritual fruit called service. Without love, it would be impossible to reach out in service to others, especially the unlovely and rejects of society. However, pure, unadulterated, wholehearted "agape" love looks beyond the surface into the very heart and needs of others and sees an opportunity to give in service so as to bless and benefit them. True love serves with joy in order to bless, enrich, encourage, and improve others.

Love was the hallmark of the life and ministry of Jesus. He set the standard of loving service during His earthly ministry, even during the worst hours of His struggles leading up to His trial and execution. Jesus was full of the Father's love from the beginning to the end, and exhibited it constantly to everyone around Him, including His disciples, enemies, and those who came just for food. Just look at a few of the verses declaring His love for His disciples:

(1) "Now before the Feast of the Passover, Jesus

knowing that His hour had come that He should depart out of this world to the Father, having **loved His own** who were in the world, **He loved them** to the end." [Jh. 13:1]

(2) "There was reclining on Jesus' breast one of His disciples, **whom Jesus loved**." [Jh. 13:23]

(3) "Just as the Father has loved Me, **I have** also **loved you**; abide in My love." [Jh. 15:9]

(4) "This is My commandment, that you love one another just as **I have loved you**." [Jh. 15:12]

(5) "The Father himself loves you" [Jh. 16:27]

These verses are incredible because they speak of His undying love for you and me. Look further at Mark 10:21 where it says that Jesus "felt a love" for the rich man who would not let go of his wealth in order to serve Him wholeheartedly. For the rich man, it was Jesus or money. Jesus knew that he needed to experience and live in God's loving will, but still, He allowed him to continue to walk in the security of his wealth, which would soon evaporate. This is a sad commentary on human life when God confronts a human being with the opportunity to receive His eternal riches only to have them reject Him and His true wealth.

Also, look at Lazarus who had died. His sisters pressed their hope in Jesus by sending Him a message saying, "Lord, behold, he whom You love is sick" [John 11:3]. Mary and Martha knew Jesus loved him in a special way, so maybe He would do something extraordinary to redeem the loss they were experiencing. In these and other situations, Jesus' love overflowed in power, wisdom, and encouragement to bless, redeem, restore, and help those in need. And in this instance He "wept" because of the deep loss that He personally felt, as well as the loss felt by the sisters. Jesus knew He would raise him from the dead, but momentarily He felt the sting of death and its temporal victory over a friend.

Love was the cornerstone of His ministry outreach to all people. He lived in the Father's love and did everything out of the richness of His love. Now that He has ascended to heaven to direct the affairs of earth, He has left us with His command to love just as He has loved, unconditionally, wholeheartedly, and fully. But there is a special love that we are to exhibit to one another in the faith. When we do that, then we will be witnesses of the Father's love between us, and will show the world that they fall far short of God's true love. Furthermore, as servant leaders, our love should reach into even the areas of sin that need to be corrected in our life and others. Too many believers take grace for granted today, and have abused this spiritual position. Unfortunately, the leaders of Christendom are falling from grace and losing the battle for the hearts and minds of millions in the world. It is up to you and me to restore the true measure of His love by loving as well as disciplining those that have misused their position of authority and defamed the name of Christ in and outside of the church.

Furthermore, we are to reproduce His love in and through our life just like Jesus. For example:

- Because Jesus loved His Father, therefore, He can command us to love the Father;

- Because Jesus loved His enemies, therefore, He can command us to love our enemies;

- Because Jesus loved His neighbor, therefore, He can command us to love our neighbors.

- Because Jesus loved His disciples, therefore, He can command us to love one another also.

Christian love is not blind, but sees the whole reality just as Jesus did. For example, Jesus loved Judas though He knew from the beginning that he would betray Him. Yet, His love was more powerful than Judas' evil and He continued to serve Judas with love up to the very end. What Jesus saw in Judas was not a betrayer, but a person created in God's image who had decided to follow his fleshly passions rather than the Lord. Judas was badly damaged by his own sin and was so self-centered that he could cover up even the small bit of godliness in himself. Still, Jesus loved him like the others through the entire 3 years of discipleship, never sending him away, but allowing him to leave when he so chose.

Christ-like love is amazing. It remains constant no matter what the circumstances are. It doesn't change because people change. And it remains focused on the person more so than the acts of the flesh. Jesus said that, "If you love me, you will keep My commandments," [John 14:15]. We know that all of His commandments are healthy for our spirit, mind, and body. But, too often we choose to follow our own will and ways, to our detriment. Therefore, if we say we love Him, then we must:

(1) Know His word thoroughly,
(2) Understand how His word applies to our daily lives, and
(3) Live out His commandments in and through our life.

Love, to be called love, has to be seen in action more so than heard in words. Hence, Christian love takes His words seriously at all points and seeks to live them out even when doing so is hard and uncomfortable. Love goes much deeper than any emotions because it goes to the very heart of a person where commitments and decisions are forged and fulfilled. True love is demonstrated through practical and useful acts because we are to 'have the love of God in ourselves.'

Love is not always easy to live out, especially when the negative emotions control or continue to dominate our feelings. Paul states that the "love of God has been poured out within our hearts through the Holy Spirit who was given to us" [Romans 5:5]. If we have the Holy Spirit, He is constantly pouring Himself, that is, His love into us. We can resist His love and the promptings that it brings, but He will not stop trying to form His will in us. We need a never-ending source of God's love in order to face the people and world around us. It is not always a friendly environment that we live in, but it can be a love-filled environment even in the face of evil if we will allow His love to flow out of us.

Life comes down to simple choices that we make. Every choice has a consequence, either good or bad. If we choose to follow His will, our choices open the doors of His heart. Consequently, His love will flow into and through us to touch others with the same measure of love with which He has touched us. If we choose to reject His will, our choices leave us in a very vulnerable place where we are trying to live in our own strength without His love, which is futile.

Love is life's greatest and best choice. He loved us while we were yet His enemies, so He willingly chose to do what was unnatural. Frankly, we stunk spiritually and yet He chose to love us anyway. Personally, I think that you and I would have had a very difficult time loving someone like ourselves, because we can only see the negative and no positive. This commitment on His part, that is, to love us anyway, became the difference in our life that brought us to salvation in the past. Because He can redeem even the foulest sinner around, He can still redeem even our greatest sins and mistakes today. His love touched our pains and healed them. His love touched our hidden places and gave us a new start in life. So why can't we trust Him to do the same now with any and all of our sins and mistakes today? A million-dollar question, with a million-dollar answer.

We could never ask for more love from Him; therefore, because He has, and is, pouring His love into us, we are to lead in this full measure of love already dwelling in us.

Principles of Leading as a Servant

Jesus came as a servant to lead the nation of Israel back to God. This was a noble cause, but unfortunately, most resisted His calling and teaching. However, He set the stage for the future Apostles to lead the Gentile world back to the One True and Living God, and their success is recorded for us in the Scriptures and church history. Today's context may be different from the first century, but we too are called to serve others so that they will return to Him who can redeem and restore what has been lost and destroyed. Our nation stands on the brink of moral collapse; politicians do not have any moral authority, business leaders have lost their moral authority, and the church leaders are now losing their moral authority because of the many sordid scandals that have unveiled decades of immorality and ungodliness. In this section we will learn the principles of hope for restoring a lost nation through servant leaders who are totally dedicated to serving and leading according to His principles.

Leadership is not a natural function for most believers,

though it really should be. In the beginning, God created Adam and Eve to lead and serve by caring for the creation under His anointing. As long as they fellowship with Him in the light, their serving and leading was more than adequate for the situation. However, when they decided to act on their own without seeking His covering and counsel, they abdicated their role and responsibility to Satan. It would be easy to condemn them by saying that they were deceived, but that can hardly be the case. God had created them perfect with knowledge and discernment of what to do and not do, so they were willingly led astray. Hence, they chose independence by rebelling against God's will and ways, costing humanity incredible devastation ever since. However, the Father's love was much stronger than the sin, so He sent Jesus to redeem us from our ongoing sin and rebellion. Through Christ He began the process of restoring our rightful role, authority and responsibility over the earth and we are to continue it everyday of our life as rightful servant leaders in His kingdom.

Key Principle of this section

Most of the examples of the principles listed below dealt with leaders in the New Testament. However, the root principles can apply to all believers whether they are servant husbands or wives, servant parents, servant children, servant workers, servant pupils, servant elders, servant factory workers, etc.

Servant leaders may not be accustomed to leading others since service is our first calling. But, each servant leader can learn to walk in the leadership roles Jesus assigns to us, whether it is on the job, in school, at home, or wherever we are part of a gathering. Too often believers do not want to step out in front to lead others because they would rather let someone else take the burden and heat that comes from being a leader. Yet, that is not a true option for us; when He calls us, we are commanded to lead others as He would. It is our God-given responsibility to take hold of life's situations and go forth as leaders into His harvest wherever that may be. If we do not, then I will guarantee you that the unrighteous and ungodly will step up to the plate and lead many astray, including some believers, in the wrong direction with the wrong convictions and wrong outcomes. The unrighteous have no choice because they lead according to their fallen nature, into darkness apart from Christ. Look at our culture today; there is incredible immorality penetrating every aspect of our society. But, no matter what area of life you look at, be sure that their leading will bring about moral, spiritual, intellectual, cultural, educational, governmental, and relational death just as starters. So lay aside any timidity and stand firm as we are commanded to do in Ephesians 6:10. Paul knew that the beginning point is our relationship with Christ was, "Finally, be strong in the Lord and in the strength of His might." Once that relationship is grounded and strong, then we can war against the spiritual powers of darkness that overshadow and negatively influence most elements of our culture. But not to worry, victory is always at hand. It is assured if and when we, the body of Christ, stay the course of righteousness till victory is won. It requires effort, patience and unity if we want to achieve His will.

Furthermore, leadership requires conviction, moral fortitude, and a genuine sense of knowing where you are going and what you need to do. In this muddled world we live in, many people would rather have a weak, non-directive, and popularly elected leader than one who is bold, assured, and steadfast. Jesus wants you as a leader, even if the world does not. Nevertheless, He wants you to love others just as He did. He also wants you to be gentle, not weak. He wants you to be the one who can give clear directions, not muddled thoughts; one who is secure in who they are, not confused by the world's changing role models; and one who will stand for truth in grace without compromise, even when the times are tough. Therefore, it will be helpful to carefully examine the New Testament principles of leadership in order to lead as He did. A servant leader should fulfill the following:

1. **Servant leaders should know where to lead God's people.** Too many so-called leaders are leading God's people down a dark alley, and there are many spiritual, moral, and ethical minefields that many will fall into. Likewise, there is a world of difference between one who is a true shepherd and one who is a hireling. Good servant leaders do not lead others into or towards temptation, but protects their sheep and themselves from temptations, as well as moral and spiritual traps [Matt. 6:13]. A servant leader is wise and discerning, that is, able to read people and the circumstances that they find themselves in. They can see and sense spiritual, moral, and ethical danger that lurks in the darkness around us. Hence, a godly servant leader guards their own heart first [Prov. 4:23], so that they can properly, effectively, and fully guard God's people from dangers and lead them in the right direction [Acts 20:28] .

2. **Servant leaders do not want or even focus on having titles** [Matt. 23:10]. A true leader does not need a title to lead or serve. Titles, in and of themselves, have no special value because it is the person, not the title, who carries the power and authority. No title will ever give anyone power and authority. Besides, titles are the badges of the world, not the Kingdom of God. Jesus

told His disciples not to be called "Father," because there is only one Father of all. He also commanded the disciples not to be called even a "leader," because He is the only true leader [Matt. 23:8-10]. Jesus said to focus on being a servant because that is the way to greatest [v. 11]. The antidote is that when a servant leader humbles himself by rejecting titles, then God will exalt him to a place of authority in His kingdom [v. 12]. So once again we see that Jesus does exactly the opposite of what the world would do.

3. **Servant leaders must be led by the Holy Spirit** [Luke 4:1; Rm. 8:14; Gal. 5:18]. Praise God that the Holy Spirit sees all things and knows how we can best serve others. Hence, the Spirit must lead us so that we can lead others in the same spirit that Jesus led His first disciples, that is, a servant spirit. It is all too easy to move forward in our own wisdom and strength without taking time to confer with the Holy Spirit. When we move too quickly, we may not be sure that we are walking in His will, which is a serious problem. A servant leader is humble, being dependent upon the Holy Spirit; slowly it will become a more natural mode to operate in, though it may not be so easy at the beginning. When you study the life of Jesus and Paul, they easily moved and ministered because they knew the Spirit and His leading. In Paul's life, as recorded in the book of Acts, twice it is mentioned that the Spirit stopped him from going where he wanted because he was moving in the wrong direction [Acts 16:6-7]. We can be sure that Paul knew the restraint of the Holy Spirit, and when we are moving against His will, we too will sense a grip on our spirit to stop and change directions. As a servant leader, it is important to walk in His peace that guides us along life's path.

4. **Servant leaders are to be examples for others to imitate, both in attitude and actions** [Luke 22:26]. In this day of political and ecclesiastical scandal, there aren't too many worthy examples to follow anymore. However, as a servant leader, we can and we must set a higher standard of morals, ethics, truthfulness, and love. When we do, God will give us a natural influence and authority with others that will bless and benefit them richly. I am convinced that people are looking for examples to follow, and their cry is to find those who can stand the test of time and oppression by the culture. Oftentimes liberals will attack those who stand for principle in the loving power of the Holy Spirit, but He will give them the ability to stand firm at all times. Three times Paul tells us to "stand firm," that is, endure under the pressure until we have won each victory [Eph. 6:11-14]. Hence, a servant leader is exposed to a great deal of attack from the world, but He will enable each of us to stand up under the pressure until our enemies are scattered.

5. **Godly servant leaders take the time to scout out the "spiritual terrain" before leading their followers**. Too often followers tend to wander spiritually, but godly servant leaders help to keep them on track. Godly leaders do not lead their followers astray from the truth or person of Jesus Christ. They have carefully evaluated the times and stepped ahead of the followers so that they do not fall into the wrong traps, such as forming wrong judgments [John 7:12 & 47]. In our day, there are so many attacks against believers that it is all too easy to fall into the trap of getting angry and striking out in judgment against others, including those inside and outside of the church.

6. **Servant leaders know God's will and ways**. This is important so that they can guide and direct people out of every spiritual, moral, intellectual, and physical bondage into the fullness of spiritual life as a servant who in turn can lead others [John 10:3; Acts 7:36]. Servant leaders by calling, as well as by necessity, must give direction to others, but it should be given in an attitude of gentleness, love, and compassion. Servant leaders see some of the future, and they want to help others avoid the pitfalls and traps that so easily entangle people in this world and culture. Jesus said that even though we are in the world, we still are not of the fallen culture that draws people away from Christ. The temptations to fall into the pattern of the non-Christian world are there, but a good servant leader knows that and guides followers away from it. Therefore, He prayed that the Father would "keep them from the evil one" in the world where we live, minister, and fight the good fight [John 17:15].

7. **Servant leaders have responsibility for finances**. This is true in the church, at home and everywhere [Acts 11:30]. However, the foundation of this principle begins in the home. Every servant leader should learn this principle at home with their own personal finances so that they may effectively practice it in the church. Every ministry needs finances to function, grow, and build its vision, and it is normal for the leaders to set the direction and priority of the funds for which they have oversight. This principle applies not only to church leaders, but also to every area of life for servant leaders. Therefore, they not only have responsibility for the general direction, but especially to funnel the funds in that direction.

8. **Servant leaders should function in plurality in decision-making** [Acts 14:23]. From the beginning of the early church, decisions were often taken by the leadership team as led by the Holy Spirit. Seldom were decision make unilaterally unless specifically called forth by the Holy Spirit. Usually leaders operated as teams and made decisions together. This principle can protect a leader from going off on a wild tangent or seeking to lord their authority over others. It is true that God gives visions to individuals, not committees or groups. But it is also true that teams can confirm a decision as from the Lord or not.

9. **Servant leaders are called upon to resolve theological disputes**. When questions, disagreements, and issues that arise between believers, between believers and the world, and contemporary issues that come up, servant leaders are to be able to solve them [Acts 15:2-6, 22-23]. The primary foundation of the Christian faith is truth, which, to be effective, must be undergirded by love and anointed by His power. The world has sought to undermine the church's foundation by changing the truth as Paul speaks about in Romans 1. However, servant leaders are to keep believers and the world on the track of truth.

10. **Servant leaders should be trustworthy and recognized for their abilities and ministry results** [Acts 15:22]. Servant leaders are given talents and opportunities. Therefore, they must be responsible, faithful, honest, and dependable in the use of their talents and opportunities. When they are, this is a sign of maturity, and the maturer they are, the more He will entrust to their care and future. Also, servant leaders are to work with key leaders, like Apostles, in their ministries

[Acts 16:4]. Servant leaders work well under divine authority; therefore, they are to work with leaders in their community such as pastors, apostles, evangelists, and others.

11. **Servant leaders are to hear ministry reports from those that have been sent out** [Acts 21:18]. This actually has several key benefits. A) The leaders can determine whether or not their investment in a ministry outreach is consistent with the goals of their church. B) They can also determine whether or not the person(s) sent out fits into the outreach ministry. Since leaders have oversight of those they are in charge of, it is critical that leaders keep closely in touch with those on the mission field, whether locally, nationally, or internationally.

12. **Servant leaders function as spiritual gifts to the body** [Eph. 4:11]. Every leader is a gift to bless and benefit others, but they are servant gifts which should keep them humble. As Paul says in I Thess. 5, we should "appreciate those who diligently labor among you" and "esteem them very highly in love" [verse 12]. Leaders function as change agents for believers when they are fulfilling their gifting and calling. Likewise, we should "obey" and "submit" to them so that they will perform their functions "with joy and not with grief, for this would be unprofitable for you" [Heb. 13:17].

13. **Servant leaders must repair, train, and equip other believers to serve and minister** [Eph. 4:11]. Every leader is called to evaluate the condition of those under their charge, to repair what is damaged in their life, and to help prepare them for ministry. Whether it is in the

family or on the job or in the church, leaders have a key responsibility to move believers into ministry. One of the reasons the church is less effective today than before is the lack of training for the general believers. Personally, I believe that every church should be a ministry-training center to develop all believers into the full God-given potential that they have so that they can touch and transform cities and nations.

14. **Servant leaders should see the results of their ministry by developing solid believers** [Eph. 4:11-16]. When leaders serve others by repairing, training, and equipping them for service, they should see a resulting increase in the number of believers who are serving, as well as an increase in the effectiveness of the overall ministries in the home or church. Likewise, when they do not see such increases, then a leader needs to take stock of what they are doing, and whether they are fulfilling God's will or not. Results should be obvious to all.

15. **Servant leaders are to lead, preside, or rule over their followers, and to care for them with diligence** [Rm. 12:18; cf. I Thess. 5:12]. Too many leaders have slacked off from their God-given responsibilities to be diligent in their service to others. Leaders are to be conscientious, hardworking, and thorough in their labor. However, one big reason this does not happen is because the church does not pay most of its leaders. For example, Paul said that leaders are "worthy of double honor" which includes the idea of paying them for their service. Plus, Peter says that a leader should not labor "for sordid gain, but with eagerness" implying that they are to be paid for their ministry [I Tim. 5:17 & I Peter 5:2].

16. **Servant leaders have responsibility for the safe-keeping of believers under their care** [I Thess. 5:12 & 14]. Whenever He places us in a leadership position, Paul says we are to teach and correct those who are unruly; discipline all for their good, as well as help the weak and hurting. A good servant leader knows the condition of those in their charge and how best to serve them so that they will grow in grace, character, truth, as well as ministry. Servant leaders pour themselves into those under their care so that they can grow into the full measure of Christ.

17. **Servant leaders are to discipline unruly members** [I Thess. 5:12]. Servant leaders may find this rather difficult, but it is essential. Today, we live in a culture where believers move from one church to the next and from one event to the next. There is an inherent instability within the Christian community. However, a servant leader recognizes that each member must be connected somewhere, beginning in the family. Discipline should always be done in love with the view of bringing a believer into the abundant relationship with Christ to gain the fullness of His life. In short, a servant leader is like a doctor whose diagnosis says that there is a cure, but an operation is imperative to guarantee health. Hence, a servant leader carefully and skillfully takes out the cancer so that healthy cells will grow.

18. **Servant leaders are to maintain peace among believers** [I Thess. 5:13]. Peace is not the mere absence of conflict, but it is an inner quality of spirit that is lived out in the soul and body. Peace is derived from an open and honest relationship with the Lord; where peace is absent, the relationship suffers. Therefore, a servant leader seeks to serve others by

bringing them into a living and consistent relationship with Christ. The servant leader helps others to understand the nature of that relationship and how to maintain a healthy relationship. Peace is incredibly important for all believers, especially in this topsy-turvy world we live in. Plus, genuine peace strengthens believers' bonds with one another, which in turn will help us to reach out and serve others.

19. **Godly servant leaders are to maintain godly disciplines in their life** [2 Thess. 3:11]. Too much emphasis is put on developing the body and less on developing the spirit and mind. Jesus said that we are to love Him with **all** of our spirit, soul, mind, and body. Of the three occurrences where this command occurs [Matt. 12:34ff; Mark 12:28ff; Luke 10:25ff], only once does Jesus say to love the Lord with our body, but in all three He says that we are to love Him with our heart [spirit], soul, and mind. The servant leader realizes that there are priorities to our disciplines and that we should take care of our body; but it is more important to take care of our spirit, soul and mind first. Servant leaders set the example of how to love God and our neighbors with our spirit, soul, and mind for others to see, learn, and replicate.

20. **Servant leaders must exhibit godly qualities in all of their relationships before they qualify as a leader** [I Tim. 3:1-5, 12; 5:17]. Husbands and parents are leaders simply because of their position, but in other instances they must be chosen to lead by others. In I Tim. 3, a leader must meet certain qualifications that involve key relationships with others: family, business, community, and church. If they do not have good relationships in these areas, then they are not qualified to

lead and serve others. Our life is primarily relationships, therefore we need to know how to serve others as leaders rather than command them as autocrats. A good servant leader will continually build quality relationships just as Jesus did.

21. **Servant leaders must be above reproach.** This principle applies to all situation, especially from those closest to the believer, including family, friends, church members, business associates, neighbors, enemies, and so forth [I Tim. 3:2 & 10]. Also, they must be above any charges or accusations brought against them so that even if someone tries to defame them, it will fall flat because it lacks credibility [I Tim. 5:19]. Servant leaders are not immune from sinning or making mistakes, but that should not appear as a habit for them. As a principle, servant leaders should be holy and blameless as Paul says in Eph. 1:4.

22. **Servant leaders can only have one wife** [I Tim. 3:2 & 12]. In today's world, this is not well received. In fact, many Christian denominations accept divorce as normal, and even healthy in many instances. However, you have to do some hermeneutical gymnastics to get around Paul's clear statement: "An overseer, then, must be...the husband of one wife..." [I Tim. 3:2]. Some have said this means one wife at a time. But in verse 12 of the same chapter Paul writes, "Let deacons be husbands of only one wife..." Now no one argues here that this means one wife at a time; it is clearly only one wife. This may be one of the most rejected statements in all of the New Testament! But God has a clear reason for this requirement: if a husband cannot be faithful to, or manage his marriage and family life well, then he is not qualified to be a leader of others. It's that

simple. This is the creation order restored through Jesus Christ; if we destroy it again through disobedience, then we will only undermine our authority as servant leaders.

23. **Servant leaders should be dignified in their attitudes and actions** [I Tim. 3:8]. The word "dignity" in this verse means one who is reputable or trustworthy, or one who carries a higher standard than the world, which should be true of all servant leaders. This "dignity" should not only be in our family life, but in our businesses, workplaces, our schoolwork, relationships, in our finances, our giving, our church life, and so forth. A servant leader, who has dignity, shows a healthy respect for Christ and His law as well as for others. Dignity naturally spills over into how we treat others and how we handle our Christian stewardship.

24. **Servant leaders should serve well in their positions** [I Tim. 5:17; cf. 3:13]. Paul emphasizes that a leader must perform their duties with excellence. Of course, this should apply to all believers, not just those who are leaders. A servant leader is given a position of authority not for their glory or benefit, but primarily for the benefit of those they are to serve. Therefore, a servant leader needs to know what their duties are and to do their best in carrying them out.

25. **Good servant leaders are more than decisions-makers, they are regularly engaged in "good deeds"** [Titus 3:8 & 14]. Paul speaks not only about the necessity of laboring for the Lord, but he qualifies the type of work that needs to be performed: it must be "good." The word "good" speaks to the quality and character of the work. The Lord wants our work to be inherently

good, honorable, and distinguished from the average worker. Something that is average cannot be considered excellent. So the servant leader should be known for their excellent work. Finally, Paul says that we are to "engage" in good deeds, which simply means that you and I must practice diligence in whatever we do. This will be a calling card for every servant leader.

26. **Servant leaders are to teach the Word of God thoroughly to all believers** [Heb. 13:7]. "Be transformed by the renewing of the mind. Set your mind on these things. Let the Word of God richly dwell within us; let your mind dwell or think upon these things; be of sound mind, and be renewed in the spirit of your mind" [Rom. 12:2; Col. 2: 23 & 3:16; Phil 4:8; 2 Cor. 5:1; Eph. 4:23]. All of these verses speak about the importance of using the mind to learn the Word [logos] of God. One of greatest shortcomings of the church today, and believers in general, is their lack of knowledge of the Bible. It is appalling how little of the Word of God believers know, and even less that they can live out in their lives. Servant leaders are to set the standard by loving God with **their entire** mind, but studying to demonstrate that love by teaching others. When servant leaders do that, He will naturally give us more insight into His Word and illumine more of His truth for our life and ministry.

27. **The servant leader's life should evidence (a) the fruit of the Holy Spirit, and (b) the fruit of ministry** [Heb. 13:7]. We are to "imitate" the faith of those who lead us. Therefore, a good servant leader will recognize their responsibility to bear spiritual fruit in their personal life and ministry. It is imperative that servant leaders have this balance because we are to be models that others can

see God's life in and find worthy of imitation.

28. **Servant leaders are to cover, care for, and watch over the souls of the saints** [i.e., abstain from sleep, be attentive to the spiritual condition of their flock] [Heb. 13:17]. This is probably the hardest task that any servant leader will face. Whether they are a husband or wife, parents, church leader, employer, educator, or whatever position a servant leader may hold, watching over one's followers is time consuming, emotionally draining, and demanding. A servant leader lives between two poles: leadership and servanthood. Each servant leader will feel pulled in one or the other direction.

29. **There is an interesting balance for leaders and members to find.** As examples, members are commanded to obey and submit to their leaders because He has called and gifted them to be leaders. On the other side of the balance, good leaders must also learn to lead from a position of a servant, with humility and gentleness. [Heb. 13:17]. Likewise, servant leaders need to learn respect for authority by obeying and submitting to the authorities in their life as well. However, a key reason for submitting to and obeying leaders is because they diligently labor among the saints, and maintain a worthy character in the midst of an unworthy culture.

30. **Servant leaders should have joy in their ministry to the flock, not grief** [Heb. 13:24]. Followers may or may not realize how much havoc they can cause to a servant leader's life, family, and ministry. In today's culture, it has been extremely sad to see so many self-centered "followers" who have caused divisions, confusion, and conflict within His body. Servant leaders,

like the apostle Paul, must deal with these types of followers according to Matthew 18. This is the most joyless part of being a servant leader, but it is an essential part. If the servant leader does not stop the spiritual cancer spreading through these bad influences, it will ultimately undermine and kill a leader's zeal, desire to minister, and ministry.

31. **Servant leaders should regularly pray for those in their care who are sick, and the servant leader should expect healing** [Jam. 5:14]. James qualifies the type of servant leader who will see miraculous answers to their prayer: they must be righteous. You might say, "But I'm not holy or perfect by a long shot." That is not the point. To be righteous simply means to conform to what God expects as revealed by His Word. A servant leader is self-motivated to follow God's will even though he or she will sin or fail from time to time, they are still laboring continually without any overall and persistent deficiency in their life and character.

32. **Servant leaders must accept that suffering is normal.** Suffering is normal for servant leaders in a fallen world, that is, verbal and physical abuse from others, including followers. It is part and parcel of their calling and ministry [I Pt. 5:1]. Peter says, "For you have been called for this purpose, since Christ also suffered for you, leaving you an example for you to follow in His steps" [I Pt. 2:21]. Suffering is not enjoyable, nor should it be sought after. However, because righteousness exposes unrighteousness, we should expect a natural backlash from those who would rather wallow in their sin than humbly accept His rebuke and repent. Suffering exposes our flesh to pain, but it also exposes our emotions, mind, and spirit. When this happens, we

learn very quickly where our weak points exist in our spiritual armor. When we can accept suffering as normal and endure under it till we go through to the other side, then we will know that we have matured to the level that we can do extremely great things for the Lord.

33. **Servant leaders are to shepherd their flock**. All servant leaders have followers, whether it be at home, on the job, in a school, at church, or wherever, they are to serve voluntarily and not under compulsion [I Pt. 5:2]. Servant leaders are chosen by the Lord to serve others. Serving includes teaching and equipping them to face all types of situations, problems, and dangers, as well as to oversee the flock in a general way by guiding them into the place where they are most useful.

34. **Servant leaders are to enthusiastically and willingly lead the flock, with no expectation of financial gain** [I Pt. 5:2], though they should be paid for their service [cf. I Tim. 5:17]. The focus of any servant leader should be on giving all they can to others and not on gaining what they can for themselves. Focus is very important to a servant leader because they will face many followers who are self-absorbed. Therefore, a servant leader's first priority is people and not material gain. Besides, people are part of His eternal perspective and money is part of the temporal world we live in.

35. **Servant leaders are to be examples to the flock, and should not dictate behavior or beliefs to the sheep** [I Pt. 5:3]. Of course, sometimes it would be quicker if we could simply say you must do or believe this and

that would be that. But in reality, that's not possible. We live in a time when independence has become more and more a part of our culture. Servant leaders should be prophetic voices to the body of believers and the world at large. However, we must respect each person's conscience and freedom to choose what they want to do and believe. It is disheartening to see people make wrong choices after warning them, but that becomes their choice. However, servant leaders must have a heart like a parent for their followers; you teach, you guide, you correct and love, but in the end, as they grow up in the faith, you must release them to the consequences of their own choices. This is not an easy thing to do, but sometimes experience is the best teacher, unfortunately.

36. **Servant leaders are to be subject to one another in all humility** [I Pt. 5:5]. Servant leaders need each other, and we can learn from one another. No one servant leader has all the grace, knowledge, or know-how to fulfill God's will. He has made us one part of a huge body, and as the body constantly interacts with itself, we must regularly interact with one another in order to remain healthy, vibrant, and focused on His vision and will.

37. **Finally, servant leaders should be the first to lead in the worship of Christ** [Rev. 4:4]. We will be spending eternity with Him, celebrating who He is and all that He had ever done. Therefore, being a servant leader means worshipping while at work, in our relationships, and through the use of our possessions. Worship is our expression of adoration of Him for everyone and everything that comes into our life.

These principles of leading, as a servant, should enable you to grow into the greatest servant leader possible day by day.

Applying these Principles Practically

Each of these 37 principles can be applied to your home life, school, place of employment, church, community activities, special events and so on. Simply take the root principle and allow it to operate in the life of the person who is the leader in that situation. For example, #37 above should be taken seriously by the parents in leading their children in worship at home first and foremost.

Practicing Leadership
as a Servant

Leadership from a servant's perspective is a unique approach to leadership. Every other school of thought approaches leadership from a position of dominance and not service. Most leadership models focus on control and power, rather than serving. Therefore, the servant leader is remarkably suited for believers as they seek to transform the world around them. Furthermore, it has been naturally ingrained in you and me to lead from a position of strength "above others" rather than to lead as a servant "below others". To make the transition from a worldly-minded leader to a leader who serves others will take significant time and effort on our part, but in the end it will be very rewarding for all.

Another problem that believers face today is that some popular Christian authors have simply taken worldly or business principles and "Christianized" them, rather than challenge their core principles. With this approach, the basic non-Christian core remains intact, though it has been coated with some Christian ideas. Sadly, many Christians don't even realize this and don't seem to know the difference between Christian principles and principles that have been Christianized. Too many believers simply accept what is being said and written without looking at the core values rooted in these principles. For example, when an author writes, "if you learn these leadership principles, then others will follow you," is this a truly Christian principle? Or when it is written that a leader must gain the full consent of all others before proceeding, is this a truly Christian principle? Would Paul have followed this principle? If the Holy Spirit had told him to move and his colleagues were not in 100% agreement, would he have waited? In Acts 21, this precise thing happened: a prophet took Paul's belt and prophesied by the Holy Spirit that he would be bound and delivered to the Gentiles. Then the leaders and local residents "began begging him not to go up to Jerusalem" [vv. 11ff]. But Paul knew the Holy Spirit's principle, and proceeded to follow Him even if there was not 100% backing from the others.

These theories certainly sound proper and would seem to accomplish a great deal more than moving on without a consensus. But, did Jesus ever seek a consensus from the 12 before proceeding? Hardly! He sought the Father who guided Him by the Holy Spirit and carried out His will. Keep in mind that God gives visions to individuals, not committees or groups. It is incumbent upon every follower to examine a vision in order to know if it is from God, and if it is, then to follow the one whom God has anointed with that vision. With the church losing its moral authority in our culture, as well as sacrificing many of the basic biblical principles concerning fidelity in marriage and sexual orientation, seeking consensus simply means finding the lowest common denominator, which has brought much of the church down to the world's level. Furthermore, when a leader says that they will not move on until everyone accepts their vision, is this a Christian ideal or something more hideous?

Can you imagine the apostle Paul stopping his mission to the Gentile world until the Jerusalem apostles had accepted his vision of reaching them? Again, God never gives a vision to a group or committee, but to individuals who have a heart for serving Him and His will. This principle is acknowledged throughout Scripture from the beginning to end. We must be very careful not to let the world's principles seep into our belief system or ways, otherwise we will be sowing the seeds of future corruption of Christian leadership and its attempts to transform the world around us. Remember, Jesus said that we are "in the world, but not of it." Likewise, He also said to love the Lord our God with "all of our mind;" Paul carried this point further by saying, "be transformed by the renewing of our minds." Leaders who serve use their minds to think things through rather than accepting whatever comes along or simply flowing with the crowd. Therefore, it will be crucial to elucidate some of the basic ways to lead as a servant.

Practicing leadership as a servant is more of an attitude than an action. It is not an easy task to lead with a servant's attitude, especially in the culture we live in today. Christian leadership has lost much of its resilience due to the gradual adoption of non-Christian principles into our leadership patterns. But a leader can still serve today in a way that will change and challenge others towards godliness.

The primary way that a servant leader can lead their followers is by maintaining a godly balance between loving the people and completing their God-given task. This can be a hard balance to maintain, especially when we focus in on one of these two at a time; but, it is possible to be balanced so that we love and complete the task too. Jesus came into His ministry with a clear vision of what the Father wanted Him to do during His earthly ministry. However, He was also sent to show them the Father's love so that they would want to come into a relationship with the Father of all. As one person has said, "People are our mission." Jesus did maintain a good balance and never seemed to be too focused on the task or people alone, but on both at the same time.

Secondly, a good leader can serve their followers or co-laborers through an attitude of understanding and gentleness. Because a leader may have a clear vision of where they are going, they cannot assume that those who are following fully understand or accept their vision. In fact, many people may follow because of the excitement generated by the leader without really buying into the vision. Sometimes leaders can go to extremes by either a) rejecting their followers because they just don't get it or b) by laying aside the vision in order to focus exclusively on the people. Either approach is out of balance and needs to be carefully re-examined. Hence, it would be best for a leader to serve their followers by trying to understand why the followers may not be as wholehearted and excited about the vision as they are. A leader who is given a vision from God will have a natural zeal and enthusiasm about the vision, but that does not necessarily spill over into the followers' lives and experiences. The principle that would be helpful in this type of situation would be to be gentle with those who may not have your zeal and attempt to teach them the vision so that they can understand. Most people do not like change or change quickly; be patient and give them time and knowledge so that they can grow in their understanding of the vision and comprehend what it is and know their part. Jesus was very gentle and understanding with His disciples, though He did become frustrated at times, and on one occasion said, "Are you also still without understanding?" [Matt. 15:16]. Another time Jesus said, "Have I been so long with you, and yet you have not come to know Me, Philip?" [John 14:9]. Even the best servant leaders will become frustrated with their followers at times because they may be slow in understanding, but try to be as gentle as He was.

Thirdly, a servant leader is not a taskmaster, but a God-appointed leader chosen to lead His people into the fullness of life and ministry that He has for them. Jesus told the parable of a slave who began to beat his fellow-slaves because he believed that the master wasn't coming soon [see Matt. 24:45ff]. It is very unfortunate when a leader sees their vision as the only standard of measure that others are to follow. This type of leader assumes dominance and control over the thinking and time of others, so they spiritually beat them into submission so that they become little robots who simply follow orders. Even the army allows for the individual soldier to think on their feet rather than blindly following commands. Paul even encouraged believers to be thinkers and not dumb followers [see I Cor. 12:2 where Paul talks about "however you were led."]. A good servant leader must accept the fact that not everyone will follow them, even if they offer each follower the fullness of life in Christ. Some people are just stubborn and refuse to follow anyone, so work with those who will follow. No matter who follows, lead them and do not force them into obedience. Remember, we are in the time of grace which allows others to grow at their own rate of growth instead of some uniform rate. Also, keep in mind that a good servant leader must encourage followers to grow and move on with their life. A leader doesn't simply give out ideas in hope that others will change, but must encourage and spur others on to fulfill the full potential in them. As D.L. Moody once said, 'the world has not seen what one follower can do when they fully devote themself to Christ.' To encourage means to motivate someone to do and be more than they are today. I believe that each of us would admit that there is much more in life and ministry that we could do "if" we made certain changes. However, we often refuse to implement change because of the costs we must pay. At this point, a servant leader could become so angry that they demand change just as Jim Jones did with his congregation. But on the other hand, as the world becomes more and more corrupt around us, there is an urgency that grasps a leader's heart to call for and petition the followers to implement change before it is too late. A servant leader can insist on change, but that call must be bold and gentle. When Jesus called the people to repentance, He knew what the future held, and it wasn't good. So He pleaded with the people to repent before it was too late. We live in a time and situation that says that His hand of judgment is upon this culture because of the radical rejection of God's truths. Romans 1 says that when men and women give up their "natural function" and burn with desire for one of the same sex, the "wrath of God" will be revealed. Today many so-called Christian leaders are beginning to accept the unnatural as natural. Sadly the world's principles have seeped into the church and undermined God's truth, which bring life and not death.

Furthermore, servant leaders are called to equip their followers so that they can serve God, the church and the world around them [Eph 4:11-16]. Good servant leaders realize that unequipped followers are easily led astray from Christ and His truth. This principle begins in the home where the parents must equip their children for life and ministry. However, many of us who are parents today were never equipped by our parents, so how are we to do that for our children if we don't know how? Well, the answer is simpler than you think. Jesus continually told His disciples to "abide" in His Word. In other words, live out His Word to the fullest measure. So the answer is simple: learn His Word and live out what you learn. It's that simple! In our culture there are so many demands on our time that there doesn't seem to be time to really study God's Word. Well, if that is the case for you, then you must choose to either fill your schedule with the temporal, or change it and fill it with the eternal that impacts the temporal. But what does it mean to equip someone for life and ministry? Again, the answer is not difficult. Basically, it requires three key things:

1. Knowing what to believe;
2. Knowing how to think; and
3. Knowing how to live out what you believe.

Again, it requires time to learn what to believe, think, and do. We tend to complicate things that we don't believe or want to accept. Take for example, tithing. Most Christians don't tithe, so when it is preached, they must do all sorts of spiritual gymnastics to get around the principle. It is the same here. When we are being equipped, then the new truths [which are really old but new to us because we hadn't learned them before] will challenge our present beliefs, thinking patterns, and behavior. If we continue to study His Word, we will be challenged more and more to make necessary changes in our life till we have learned a substantial part of His truth. When that happens, then the challenge to change tends to be less frequent because we are living in His truths consistently.

Equipping others is a vital fact that needs to be practiced by every servant leader for themselves and those who follow them. We can equip others only to the degree that we have equipped and lived out His truths ourselves.

A Leader is...

Knowing the qualities of a good leader will enable you to live everyday by He desires. Brief statements about your role will help you to quickly review what a leader should be. Also, you can use these short statements as prayers of commitment to being a leader like Jesus Christ. Therefore, listed below are just a few statements of what a leader is, but you should add to it and make it a personal prayer for your life and ministry. Therefore, a leader is...

Under His authority of love, compassion and mercy for all they lead...

One who leads out of love for people...

One who sees the task at hand and guides people into fulfilling His will...

One who takes seriously the call to lead others like and to Christ...

Dedicated to being the best "servant" leader possible...

One who willingly changes in order to maximize their leadership potential...

Responsible to God for leading and not just following the crowd...

One who refuses to give in to peer pressure and follow the culture...

Able to see that their influence goes far beyond what they do in the immediate...

One who takes time to learn everything they can about godly leadership...

Willing to help others grow into their full potential...

One who knows who they are in Christ, and are secure in Him...

Unwilling to get upset when they don't get their way...

Accepting of their role to watch over others under their care...

Aware that they will not get rich in their ministry as a leader...

Able to maintain Christ-like dignity in all circumstances...

Constantly learning His word, will and ways...

Fully dedicated to the life of a leader in whatever capacity He has placed them, whether at home, in the church, on their job, in school, in their community, etc. A leader accepts all responsibilities given them by Christ because His call is necessary for their life and ministry.

Part IV

Servant Leaders – They Make a Difference

Leaders who serve with
a Christ-like heart will change
the people and world around
them. The greatest servant leader
will give his or her
life for the benefit and
blessing of others.

Jesus' Leadership Style

J esus' leadership style is quite captivating when compared with other historical leaders, be they religious or
political. His leadership style was service-centered, not
self-centered. It was people-oriented, not profit-oriented.
Also, Paul, for example, was called a "task theologian"
because he developed his theology in the midst of his ministry, he was still service oriented just like Jesus. His leadership was designed to lead people out of bondage to sin,
Satan and the world's ways into a life of freedom in the
spirit, freedom in the Word, and freedom in relationship
with others. Jesus saw every individual's primary needs and
reached out to meet those needs by drawing them into a loving relationship based upon the living truth found in Him.
Truth apart from that relationship will become stale and
powerless. The Pharisees are the prime example of what
happens when you divorce truth from the relationship with
Jesus and replace it with traditions that are lifeless and cruel
in their demands.

Jesus' servant leadership was not burdensome or hard
like that of the autocratic Pharisees. When He looked at peo-

ple, He saw a person of infinite value who had strayed from their covenantal relationship with the Father, so He set out to bring each person back into that eternal and secure relationship. The woman caught in adultery was to be stoned under Mosaic Law, but when she was thrown down at His feet, He reached out in love and touched and healed her life. At the same time, He sought to serve her accusers by leading them back to the grace of God, that is, be kind, patient, and compassionate towards sinners because they too could fall as easily as she did. When He met the rich young man, He knew in advance that his life was intimately consumed by his love of money. Looking into his heart as well as his future, Jesus set out to lead him out of bondage to the inanimate money into a living relationship with the Giver of all wealth. Likewise, when He encountered Nicodemus, Jesus set out to illuminate the truth of being in a born-again relationship with the Father. Nicodemus was not too far from that relationship, but he was torn inside between loyalty to the Jewish leadership and yet sensing in his spirit that Jesus was the living truth embodied for mankind. His style of leadership set him apart from all other leaders because of His central concern for people's present and future. He was normally gentle in His confrontation, but He always coupled it with eternal truth and grace with direction how to change before it was too late.

When we compare Jesus to recent political or religious leaders, He is so different that it is almost impossible to adequately compare them. Take for example leaders like Ghandi, Hitler or Clinton. Ghandi, though a good man, attempted to use non-violent means to accomplish his desired will, that is, to push the British out of India. On the surface, this seemed like a good goal. However, it was a temporal goal without any eternal connections to the One True God. His style revealed the main problem, the results did not alleviate the centuries of pain and suffering in India, but unfortunately reaffirmed, and even enhanced it even more because he failed to deal with the underlying root problems. Ghandi's style forced a change in the political system, but he was unable to bring about a change in the caste system or religious tensions within India that continue to take the lives of hundreds, and even thousands, today.

Hitler, on the other hand, was a totally self-absorbed man who used force and coercion to make everyone follow his will and ways. He set the goal before himself to conquer Europe, and went about achieving it at all costs, even the absolute destruction of Europe if need be. Because he was the center of his world, he was unwilling to humble himself and follow better advice, thus causing the death of tens of millions of people and the literal destruction of nations and their history. And sadly he used the church as often as he could to force people to yield to his will, which was a trait of the old medieval system.

Finally, Bill Clinton is a contemporary example of a man who was very personable, but corrupt at the core of his being. He could say the right words in the right way at the right time, but then undo them by his actions. His leadership style was basically self-oriented and self-protective, though he was forced from time to time to lead in a good and acceptable way when he had no other choice. He was a glory seeker, not a servant leader.

Key Principle

Service to others is what separates Jesus from all other leaders throughout all of history. He came to serve, bless, and benefit others. Other leaders have sought to serve, bless, and benefit themselves instead of those they are over.

Jesus, on the other hand, led from a position of humility as a bondservant, owing His allegiance to the Father who called Him to live in the flesh as a servant leader, like you and me. His leadership style was for the sole benefit of those to whom He ministered, and not for Himself at all. He embodied the attitude and actions of a leader seeking to serve others, to provide the very best possible for the present and future advantage of every recipient. His service to others was founded on three key principles of life and ministry. Having:

Vision
Values
Plans

His vision was to redeem mankind and restore the creation order so that mankind could relate to God as their Father again. He saw what the world could be like if everyone would take His words seriously, because He wanted to restore the original creation plans so that mankind would rule over the earth with the grace and truth of God. But in order to accomplish that vision, He had to be out constantly in the crowds, teaching them as well as modeling for them God's vision for humanity. Jesus never isolated Himself in an ivory tower, nor did He surround Himself with a bunch of "yes men." In fact, He chose men who had imperfect natures like you and me to show that He could transform us into servant leaders like Himself.

Key Principle

A godly vision undergirded by godly values will powerfully affect others as its strategy is implemented. If one of these three elements is either missing or corrupted, the other two will fail, eventually. Therefore godliness must tie the three together in order to reach its maximum potential.

Likewise, He embodied the values of holiness that set Him apart from mankind. His values were seen in how He lived, treated others [especially sinners and the rejects of society], spoke God's words, and lived out His life in every situation. God's values are more than the Ten Commandments, but revealed in the great commandment to love God and our neighbors which He did at all times. As a model of serving and leading others, He fulfilled that commandment in every detail which set the standard for all believers to follower thereafter.

Finally, He had a very clear and simple plan: raise up disciples, bring the message of salvation to Israel, and let the disciples take it throughout the world. During His lifetime He would reach out to the lost house of Israel and no further because the Father had placed limits on His plan. He did touch a few gentiles in His ministry, but it was more often used for teaching the Jews that were in dire danger of losing His salvation. He left His disciples on earth to continually carry out His plan to reach the Jews and gentiles throughout the world. At His ascension He told them to go into the entire world and to lead others to salvation and holiness just as He did in Israel. However, they didn't get the message, so He sent a little persecution to spur them on to leave Jerusalem and go to the East, West, South, and North to tell others about Jesus. It is always interesting to see how He has to motivate us sometimes to fulfill our calling as servant leaders, but the end result is always beneficial to all.

Jesus' leadership style focused on people and eternal truth. He ministered to the needs of the people He met while challenging them to live in His Word in all areas of their life. Meeting their physical or emotional needs was not His primary goal, though it may have been essential to gain their attention and interest. His primary goal was to uncover and meet their spiritual needs; this was His heart's desire with everyone He encountered. In order to do that, the presentation of God's truth was essential to the transformation of mankind; therefore, His task was to meet people where they were and to call them to a higher level of living through repentance from evil into godliness. He laid before them a decision to make the right choices for their benefit as well as the benefit of generations to come.

Jesus was a leader from the beginning of His call. He led the way when the crowds were only interested in having their physical needs met. He led the way when He called the twelve. And He led the way when He told them the "hard truths" about being a disciple so that those who would follow Him would come with open eyes and with a full commitment. If they would follow Him as their leader, then the disciples could call others to follow Him as they were following Him.

He challenged and called everyone to follow Him, but He left the final decision to the individuals. His heart was broken over the effects of sin that He saw in so many people, but as a servant leader, He had done all He could to lead them out of bondage into God's will and ways, but that was all He could do. You and I can do the same and leave the results up to the Father which is not always easy to do, but is very freeing in spirit, mind, and body.

In conclusion, I must say that it is disheartening to see so many followers of Christ in this culture turn from the hard truths to an easy gospel of grace. Grace is a free and generous gift from God, but it is very costly to Him and us. If we are to be true servant leaders like Jesus, then we must be willing to go through the tough preparations that are necessary in order to weed out the wrong attitudes, beliefs, and behavior. Otherwise, we will not be able to stand in the times of trials that always come upon those who fully follow Him as the true leader.

Jesus' Servant Style

Jesus was a servant par excellence. He took the unique step of humbling Himself from a position of power and glory in order to enter into our world as a servant to others. Even though He was God in the flesh, He became a "bond servant" in order to demonstrate for you and me how a servant leader functions and can transform their life and others around them. He was God's change agent that began a revolution in the first century and we have carried on since through the anointing of the Holy Spirit and with the fullness of His truth.

His servant style was uncharacteristic when compared with other leaders then and now. Other leaders don't normally think about how they can serve others, but only themselves. Jesus did not come to dominate through force and power, but through the loving grace and eternal truth of God. He was dedicated to a servant's lifestyle that blessed and benefited others. For Jesus, that was not an option because He knew that serving was the only way to lead in this fallen world. This is probably the harder way to lead, but God promises that the humble servants shall inherit the earth!

For some, serving has no appeal as a leadership style because it functions from a position of weakness under others; besides, if you are under others, the possibility of being misused looms large. Furthermore, serving seems to delay the possibility of bringing about any change because a servant has no power, authority, or right to dictate to anyone. In addition, serving seems to devalue the leader and places them at a disadvantage. However, the Father knew that the world's ways could not solve any problems nor provide for the type of change that He knew was needed. A new leadership style was necessary and He chose a servant's style as the proper way to accomplish His will. It is foolishness to the wise, but even His "apparent" weakness is stronger than their greatest efforts. Jesus took the exceptional step of laying aside all of His divine prerogatives and accepted the humblest position possible in order to show that it was God who would achieve His will through that of a bondservant. You and I should take heart in this because we too can serve with the expectations that He can accomplish through us what He accomplished through Jesus and more. This is what has set Him apart from all other leaders throughout history, seeking to serve as a leader rather than control others through various means.

Jesus' style of serving others was evident from the beginning of His ministry. He constantly kept an eye on the needs of the people around Him, as well as stepped forward to minister in unexpected ways when the opportunities arose. For example, He was invited to Peter's home; upon arriving there, someone told Him that Peter's mother-in-law was ill and needed help. Immediately, He came to her aid and served her through His healing touch. Likewise, crowds seemed to follow Him wherever He went. Many came out of curiosity, some out of physical needs, and some were looking for a spiritual leader, while still others just came because of the crowds. But no matter the reason, He served the crowds by giving them spiritual food as well as actual food for their needs. He moreover served His own disciples by taking them with Him on ministry trips, by training them in various ways, as well as modeling the Truth before them. But more amazingly, He served the religious leaders who were generally loathed by the crowds and plotting against Him. Whenever He encountered them, He discerned their reason for meeting with Him, either to trap Him by a question or other situation in order to demonstrate their superiority for themselves and the crowds, or to undo His theology. Instead of falling into their traps, He often rebuked them and corrected their misunderstandings and false teachings. This in and of itself was quite a challenge, but Jesus faced it as a servant to help them see their blind spots, to confront their arrogance, and challenge them to humble themselves before God in the flesh. Not to many did that, but for those who did, His service through a rebuke was fruitful for them. Look at Nicodemus, caught between the elders of his day and a desire to be genuine in his faith, he found it hard to break off from the old patterns of living and accept the new patterns of life laid out by Jesus. He did change slowly, so Jesus served him and others like him in hopes of bringing them to salvation and a knowledge of who He was.

He served everyone He encountered through the love, grace, and truth that filled Him. God the Father wanted everyone to know, experience, and understand the full measure of His love, grace, and truth so that they would want to change and follow Him. In today's world, there are numerous religions that offer peace and truth, but none have the True Servant who can give them eternal life in addition to eternal peace, truth, forgiveness, love, and acceptance by the one true Father.

His disciples had difficulty catching on to His servant style and manner, which is also to say that you and I encounter the same difficulty. Near the end of His earthly ministry, the mother of the sons of Zebedee came to Him with a request to seat her sons at His right and left hands, that is, in the places of authority. This is the typical desire of most believes, but in order to fulfill His call upon our life, we too must lay aside all desires and expectations of leading through power and authority and accept the position of a servant as the only way to change the world.

We Are "The" Servant Leaders of Today!

Today you are the servant leader whom Jesus wants to use to change and transform others around you. You can, will, and must make a difference for the sake of your family, church, schools, work places, community and nation. Without your wholehearted dedication to serving and leading as He did on earth, the future is bleak at best. If you want your life to make a difference, learn and live the principles incorporated in this book; over time you will see a significant positive impact in your life as it touches and transforms others. If you want your church to make a difference, the believers must learn and live the principles incorporated in this book, and over time the body of Christ will see a significant positive impact in the lives of tens and hundreds of people it touches and transforms. Yes, Jesus has chosen you and enabled you to be the best servant leader possible!

He has already bought us at the price of His life; therefore, we owe Him our all. We are His property, required to serve and lead at His beckoning and to be ready to do all that He asks of us. For many this sounds too hard and unacceptable. But when you compare His yoke and commands to those of our culture, other leaders, or even our own desires, He truly is very kind with us, gentle in His ways, and patient in helping us to grow up into servant leaders.

In this final chapter, it is time to bring everything to a conclusion and personally accept the fact that He has chosen you to be a servant leader like Himself. His plan is to change the world for better through servant leaders like you, beginning with your life and home. You are one of those chosen vessels that He has called to be a servant leader after His example, and you are the one who can change your world if you follow after Him with all of your spirit, mind, and strength. However, you must take personal responsibility for making the right choice to be a servant leader like Him, keeping in mind that one day we will give an account of our life before His judgment seat. Look at the long-term impact of how change in you and me can literally affect the future and destiny of nations with millions of people:

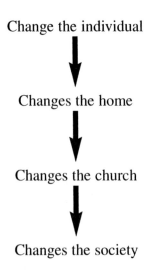

Change the individual

Changes the home

Changes the church

Changes the society

Changes the nation

Changes the future

And changes the destiny of nations!

However, the problem lies here: if there is a breakdown in the change process in the individual and home, then the nation and future is doomed to the advancing spread of evil and moral darkness. The breakdown usually occurs because believers have given up hope for change or they have tried, but have not received, any support from the Christian community. In today's world, many, if not most, of our sins are committed in private, thereby undermining our effectiveness in the public arena of life. What we are in private is revealed in public; if we commit private sins such as moral or financial failings which ultimately is self-centered, then we will commit public sins against our fellow believers by focusing in on ourselves and ignoring their needs. The long-term result of this ongoing problem is that more and more believers become self-centered in their world, which allows the unrighteous culture to advance before our very eyes. And even worse, the sins of the nation grow through our passivity. Therefore, all of this is to say that since He has chosen us to be servant leaders, we must take wholehearted responsibility for this calling upon our lives, because it will affect our generation and several after us.

Now back to the main point: You have been called as a

believer, but that is only the beginning of the exciting and abundant life He has in store for you. There is so much more to come, and each new day will bring an opportunity to serve and lead others you meet.

You have also been anointed by almighty God to serve and lead others into the abundant life that Jesus has for everyone beginning with salvation and continuing on through the spiritual growth stages of life. But salvation must be followed by an increasingly godly lifestyle that will allow you to grow in holiness, that will give you the right to lead others by serving their true needs.

However, you and I both struggle with the idea of servant leadership in our daily life because we are often pulled in one of two different directions. It seems that when we attempt to apply it to our life, then we see only more failings and darkness in our own life. This is quite normal because as we seek to change the very core of our being, then like mining for gold, you have to sift through a lot of dirt to find those valuable nuggets. Sometimes we will swing between the two poles of serving and leading, but like Jesus we should try to seek the balance so that we can walk in the security of His love, grace, and truth as we pour our lives into others.

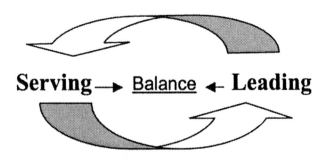

Serving ⟶ Balance ⟵ Leading

The Lord has chosen you to be a servant leader of, and for, others. That's a fact! He has gifted you with a special personality that is uniquely created for the place and time you live. And He has called you to be ready to serve those whom He sends across your path.

Jesus was always ready, willing, and able to serve and lead others because He knew He was called to do this. When we look at His life, we find two goals set before Him: (1) people who needed salvation, and (2) the task of training others to follow in His footsteps. He was called to fulfill His task within three short years because whatever foundation He laid for the future would determine the type of changes that would come through His servant leaders after Him. Yet, His calling was to serve others through His loving grace and truth.

Amazingly, He was able to keep a balance between the task set before Him and the people He was called to minister to. For us, it isn't easy. People who tend to focus too much on people often forget the task they have been called to; and those who focus on the task often forget that people are our primary ministry. Keeping a balance is difficult to maintain, but not impossible.

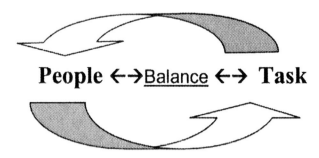

People ←→Balance ←→ Task

We are His servant leaders, chosen to be where we are at the present time to serve and lead in our generation just as He did in His. He has given us influence far beyond what the eye sees, power to carry out His will, holiness to walk in, and truth to build into our life and others. Therefore, let us serve and lead as He did, believing that our generation will be transformed just as He transformed His generation and all generations thereafter.

Part V

<u>Conclusion</u>

Servant Leadership is the most
dynamic, rewarding and exciting
life a Christian could possibly
live! Hence, A servant leader is…

A Servant Leader is...

As we come to the end of this study of servant leadership, it would be helpful to capture the function and life of a true servant leader in a few sentences. Please make these a personal ongoing prayer for your individual life and ministry so that He can make you into the best and most productive servant leader ever! Hence, a servant leader is...

One who depends totally on the Father for everything...

One who puts service before self...

Willing to lead because if they don't, the world will lead them astray...

Able to be humble, yet firm in their convictions when serving and leading...

Desiring to put people before tasks...

A person of positive spiritual influence...

One who does not seek for greatness, but opportunities to serve and lead...

Able to recognize that all glory goes to Him alone for all the good they can do...

Constantly standing apart from the crowd because they are fully dedicated to Him...

Able to accept that they can do all things through Christ who strengthens them...

Willing to stand up for what is right even when everyone else opposes them...

Able to see the possibility of positive change in everyone and every circumstance...

Willing to be wronged by others like Christ, Paul and others who were wronged constantly...

A servant leader is a unique person in the world we live in today. Serving and leading is almost unheard of outside of the Christian community, and even inside it is sometimes scoffed at or rejected. However, Jesus made it quite clear that greatness is the end result of serving others. But, sanctification is also the result of leading others. Christ is looking for Christian men and women who are willing to fully follow His will and ways of serving and leading. Therefore, step out in faith to walk with Him as a servant leader everyday of your life, impacting others through the loving truth that He pours into you for the benefit and blessing of others.

Contact information for Dr. McGeorge:

Servant Leadership Ministries

10301 Edgebrook Ct.
Richmond, VA 23235

(804) 272-7600
SLMjfmjr@aol.com
http://www.ServeLead.com

Visit Servant Leadership Ministries web site at:
http://www.Servelead.com

For more information on Dr. McGeorge's
- Speaking availability
- Training seminars and
- Books

Please contact him as follows:

Phone/fax:
(804) 272-7600

Mail:
Servant Leadership Ministries [SLM]
10301 Edgebrook Ct.
Richmond, VA 23235-3803

E-mail:
SLMjfmjr@aol.com

<u>Request to receive the Bi-monthly</u>
<u>Newsletter on Servant Leadership</u>

SLM publishes a bi-monthly newsletter on servant
leadership principles.
To receive the newsletter, contact SLM at:
Web site: **http://www.ServeLead.com**,
Guest Sign In Page, or
Call at (804) 272-7600, or
Write to 10301 Edgebrook Ct.,
Richmond, VA 23235-3803

Printed in the United States
1152500003B/64-153